Contents

Introduction to the series

The recent, rapid growth of both Film and Media Studies post-16 has inevitably led to a pressing demand for more teachers for these popular courses. But, given the comparatively recent appearance of both subjects at degree level (and limited availability of specialist post-graduate teaching courses), many new and experienced teachers from other disciplines are faced with teaching either subject for the first time, without a degree-level background to help them with subject content and conceptual understanding.

In addition, the recent post-16 specifications (syllabi) saw the arrival of new set topics and areas of study, and some of the specifications have frequently changing topics, so there is a pressing need for up-to-date resources to help teacher preparation.

This series has been developed specifically with these factors – and the busy teacher – in mind. Each title aims to provide teachers with an accessible reference resource, with essential topic content, as well as clear guidance on good classroom practice to improve the quality of their teaching and their students' learning. Every author in the series is an experienced practitioner of Film and/or Media Studies at this level, and many have examining/moderating experience.

Key features
- Assessment contexts
- Suggested schemes of work
- Historical contexts (where appropriate)
- Key facts, statistics and terms
- Detailed reference to the key concepts of Film and Media Studies
- Detailed case studies
- Glossaries
- Bibliographies
- Student worksheets, activities and resources (available online) – ready for you to print and photocopy for the classroom.

Other titles in the series include:
Teaching Scriptwriting, Screenplays and Storyboards for Film and TV Production; Teaching TV Sitcom; Teaching TV News; Teaching Analysis of Film Language and Production; Teaching TV Soaps; Teaching Women and Film; Teaching Video Games; Teaching Digital Video Production; Teaching British Broadcasting since 1990; Teaching British Cinema since 1990; Teaching Film Censorship and Controversy; Teaching Television Language; Teaching Music Videos.

SERIES EDITOR: Vivienne Clark is a former Head of Film and Media Studies. She is an Advanced Skills Teacher, an Associate Tutor of *bfi* Education and Principal Examiner for A Level Media Studies for one of the English awarding bodies. She is a freelance teacher trainer and writer/editor on Film and Media Studies, with several published textbooks and teaching resources, including two recent student textbooks, *GCSE Media Studies* (Longman 2002) and *Key Concepts & Skills for Media Studies* (Arnold 2003). She is also a course tutor on the *bfi*/Middlesex University MA level module: An Introduction to Media Education (distance learning).

Author: Kate Gamm is Lecturer in A Level Film Studies at East Surrey College in Redhill, Surrey, having also worked in the adult education sector. She is the Principal Examiner of WJEC A2 Film Studies Unit FS5: Studies in World Cinema, as well as an Associate Tutor of *bfi* Education.

Introduction

Assessment contexts

Awarding body & level	Subject	Unit code	Module/Topic
✓ AQA A2 Level	Media Studies	Module 5	Independent Study
✓ AQA A2 Level	Media Studies	Module 6	Comparative Critical Analysis
✓ OCR A2 level	Media Studies	2734	Critical Research Study
✓ OCR A2 level	Media Studies	2735	Media Issues and Debates
✓ WJEC A2 Level	Film Studies	FS4	Making Meaning 2: *Auteur* Research Project
✓ WJEC A2 Level	Film Studies	FS5	Studies in World Cinema
✓ WJEC A2 Level	Film Studies	FS6	Critical Studies
✓ WJEC A2 Level	Media Studies	ME4	Investigating Media Texts
✓ WJEC A2 Level	Media Studies	ME5	Changing Media Industries
✓ SQA Advanced Higher	Media Studies	DOYN:12	Higher Media Literacy: Film

This pack is also relevant to the teaching of film in the following specifications, as well as for Lifelong Learning and international courses:

- OCR, Ed-Excel, AQA – GNVQ and AVCE
- BTech National Diploma

The following titles in this series would be useful companions to this pack:

- *Teaching Analysis of Film Language and Production* – for a full exploration of film language and how to analyse films, as well as production methods
- *Teaching British Cinema since 1990*. This guide is particularly relevant to the AQA, OCR and WJEC A Level Media Studies specifications, and

especially WJEC's A level Film Studies specification, as well as to Scottish Highers and Advanced Highers and GNVQ and AVCE courses. It may also prove useful for undergraduates with a World cinema component in their degree course who have not taken A Level Film Studies, or who perhaps took AS Film Studies only.

● Specification links

The guide will help teachers following a specification with a European or World cinema approach. Section 2 contains an explanation of key film and media concepts and approaches that would apply across a range of films, while the case study films in Section 3 could be adapted for use with a range of other European or Third World countries.

AQA Media Studies A2 – Unit 4: Texts and Contexts in the Media
This unit supports reference to concepts such as representation, media language and forms, narrative and genre covered by this resource.

AQA Media Studies A2 – Module 5: Independent Study
Independent study allows students to go beyond the realms of the A2 specification itself into more diverse forms of media texts such as those covered in this resource.

AQA Media Studies A2 – Module 6: Comparative Critical Analysis
The specification makes reference to representation and genre, and their wider historical, social, political and economic contexts.

OCR Media Studies A2 – 2734: Critical Research Study
The information on Claire Denis, in the case study section on France, would be appropriate for independent research for the optional topic, Women and Film.

OCR Media Studies A2 – 2735: Media Issues and Debates
The resource provides a useful context for study of the optional topic on British Cinema since 1990, by focusing on features of non-Hollywood cinema study.

SQA Advanced Higher
There is scope to choose examples of World cinema in some parts of Advanced Higher, particularly in relation to comparative research projects.

WJEC Media Studies A2 – ME4: Investigating Media Texts
The specification requires students to undertake research of a media form of their choice. While this resource is aimed primarily at teachers, it could also provide guidelines for students wishing to pursue an independent study of a national cinema featured here.

WJEC Media Studies A2 – ME5: Changing Media Industries

This unit invites students to make comparisons between the British media and other national industries; the contextual background of the case study national cinemas contained in this resource may prove relevant.

WJEC Film Studies A2 – FS4: Auteur Research Project

This unit allows students to undertake independent research of an *auteur* of their choice. The guide features a number of contemporary *auteurs* whose films are likely to hold strong appeal for students: Wong Kar-Wai, Lukas Moodysson, Lars von Trier, Claire Denis, Mathieu Kassovitz.

WJEC Film Studies A2 – FS5: Studies in World cinema

The guide contains reference to a number of close study and topic area films contained on the FS5 specification. *Chungking Express* (Wong Kar-Wai, 1994, Hong Kong) is currently one of the focus films featured in the Cinematic New Waves topic, which can be considered with *In the Mood for Love* (Wong Kar-Wai, 2000, Hong Kong/France/Thailand) as a further case study film by the same director. Three more focus films on the specification featured here are *La Haine* (Mathieu Kassovitz, 1995, France), *Beau travail* (Claire Denis, 1999, France) and *Show Me Love* (Lukas Moodysson, 1998, Sweden).

These films provide case study material that can be adapted for use in other specifications. *Beau travail*, for instance, provides a good example of the work of a female director whose films do not apparently fit into the 'feminist film' category, an approach that would be of relevance to OCR A2 Media Studies Unit 2734: Critical Research Study and the topic of Women and Film.

Similarly, the case study films enable comparisons to be made with British cinema in terms of their being 'alternatives' to Hollywood, a useful approach for OCR A2 Media Studies Unit 2735: Media Issues and Debates.

WJEC Film Studies A2 – FS6: Critical Studies

As the final synoptic paper of A Level Film Studies, this unit allows for critical reflection on the course as a whole. Student work on World cinema undertaken at A2 Level in particular can be reconsidered in the light of the approaches taken by this paper. For example, the directors featured in this guide offer a different perspective for the section on genre and authorship studies. Also, issues of film censorship and debates around what constitutes the 'shocking' in cinema can be expanded upon in considering films such as *The Idiots* (Lars von Trier, 1998, Denmark/Sweden/France/Netherlands/Italy) and *Festen* (Thomas Vinterberg, 1998, Denmark/Sweden)

Getting started

There are a number of very good reasons for studying examples of World cinema, beyond the assessment requirements of various examinations. Not least is the fact that our students' experience of cinema is likely to be quite narrow, and they may not have seen a wide range of interesting and high-quality films made around the world. The majority of films screened at our local UK cinemas and multiplexes tend to be mainstream Hollywood films, with an occasional 'indie' US film, a few UK films and possibly, very occasionally, a German, French or Italian film. Hollywood's dominance tends to be reflected in what is taught in the media/film classroom – and it is important to note that this guide is not anti-Hollywood. But one of our aims is to encourage more teachers to explore the rich material found in World cinema and look for opportunities to bring such films into the classroom more frequently.

The prodigious international commercial success of *Finding Nemo* (Andrew Stanton and Lee Unkrich, 2003, USA), for example, is a testament to the financial power of Hollywood and its ability to distribute and exhibit its films globally. The result of this is that a US hit will dominate the box-office takings in many countries around the world. In any study of World cinema it is therefore important to examine the hegemonic relationship between Hollywood and national cinemas, from cultural, ideological, economic and formal perspectives.

Hollywood mainstream cinema arguably constitutes a global cinema culture. Furthermore, it tends to represent the rest of the world through a filter of US popular culture and values, producing stereotypical representations of other countries and cultures. Some commentators have identified Hollywood as an agent of cultural imperialism, alongside other global brands such as Coca-Cola, Microsoft and McDonald's, creating a monoculture, which serves to homogenise cultural difference and diversity.

A major issue in the study of World cinema is therefore the problem of defining what it actually is. One popular definition (that is commonly also used to define independent cinema) is that it is everything that isn't Hollywood, comprising the work of individual national filmmakers. However, even this simple definition is problematic as it privileges the location of the film's financial source, or the birthplace of the director, over other factors. One could equally consider other factors such as the nationality of its main creative talent, where a film is set or filmed, or its subject matter. This definition also implies that World cinema is anti-Hollywood or not populist in its appeal, which is not necessarily the case.

The issue of a film's nationality becomes further complicated, given that US film production, distribution and exhibition companies may finance projects from other countries, and that, increasingly, many films are international co-productions. Furthermore, these patterns of ownership and finance mean that it is far easier for some examples of World cinema to be seen in London, Sydney, Toronto or New York than in their country of origin.

Very closely related to issues of national cinema are those of national identity and how it is defined, represented and expressed through a film culture. What separates one nation from another, apart from its geography? Culture, religion, history, race, language? Even issues of nationality are not fixed, given the long history of economic migration and flights from oppression from one country to another. Most countries now have mixed populations with a variety of cultural heritages, each of which make their own contributions to a nation's creative industries. How does this affect our understanding of World cinema?

Furthermore, where do other English-language cinemas lie in relationship to Hollywood (eg UK, Canada, Australia and New Zealand)? What is the difference between World cinema and Third World cinema, or Third cinema for that matter? Is Hollywood the national cinema of the USA, or, as indicated above, does it constitute an international, or global, cinema, rather than representing the USA itself? It could indeed be argued that Hollywood cinema does not represent the people of the USA and their cultures. Certainly there are those filmmakers who specialise in alternative representations of the USA in their work, such as Jim Jarmusch, John Sayles, Michael Moore, Spike Lee, Alison Anders, Richard Linklater, Harmonie Korine and Vincent Gallo, among many others.

Most international filmmakers are inevitably judged (by a variety of criteria) against Hollywood mainstream cinema – what effect does the predominance of Hollywood film form have on film audiences and their expectations of a film? What happens to an indigenous culture when its film audiences watch predominantly dubbed Hollywood fare? What opportunities are there for self-representation, seeing their own faces, lives, language and experience on screen? What happens to non-US filmmakers when they make films in Hollywood or in another language – how does their nationality inform their work, or do they just conform to the narrative, stylistic and ideological expectations of mainstream Hollywood?

The above are some of the issues related to the study of World cinema and, among others, they should be considered alongside your teaching of any national cinema.

This resource is certainly not definitive – four national cinemas are featured here (Hong Kong, Sweden, Denmark and France) – but it is hoped that you will explore other national cinemas, equipped with some of the key issues for studying the topic of World cinema from this pack.

- You might find the list of World cinema directors and their countries of origin a good place to start. See the Teaching World Cinema pages of www.bfi.org.uk/tfms.

In 'Recommended further reading and viewing' (see p83) there are lists of useful books, reference sources and websites for teachers wishing to explore other national cinemas so they may develop their own case studies modelled on the ones contained here.

Availability of many films on VHS/DVD is one key resource issue in studying World cinema. This, in itself, is worth discussing with students. Major film distribution companies do not find it sufficiently profitable to make international films with English subtitles available. Smaller distributors in the USA and Europe have, however, taken advantage of the cost effectiveness of DVD technology in releasing a wider range of World cinema titles.

Examiners and moderators in Media or Film Studies are looking for, particularly at A2 and undergraduate level, a sense of personal response to, and engagement with, a topic in candidates' work. Teaching World cinema may present you with a challenge, therefore, as the films that students encounter in this topic may diverge considerably from their cinemagoing or personal experience. They may be put off by the foreign language and subtitles, and by the different stylistic features. So the initial unfamiliarity of a film's form and its spoken language might need to be addressed before students can access and engage with the subject matter.

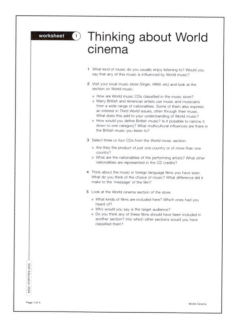

Therefore we must start with our students formulating (or challenging) ideas about what the term 'World cinema' may mean, by discussing some of the issues mentioned above. Students at A2 Level will probably have had some experience of issues around national cinemas (either of their own or of Hollywood) and/or their distribution contexts at AS Level. See **Worksheet 1**.

Having considered definitions of World cinema, students can be introduced to studies of national cinemas and film texts in the broader context of Film Studies and its associated concepts. As the term 'World cinema' really means 'every cinema of the world', ask students how they would define 'British cinema'. For example, could we say that British cinema is part of World cinema? For an American or Australian student, how would British cinema be defined? See **Worksheet 2**.

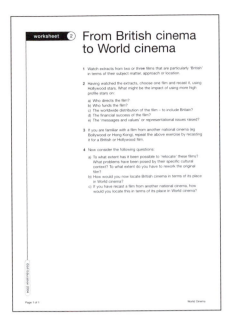

Students can then undertake some Internet research on British directors on www.imdb.com. Their findings will show a wider perspective on the profile of British films across the world, including awards and nominations at international film festivals. Film Studies students may know from their work at AS Level that British stars are defined largely by their success in Hollywood. They may be unaware, however, of the level of critical and popular success enjoyed by certain British directors in Europe and beyond, eg Ken Loach, Peter Greenaway and Mike Leigh.

For example, there is an annual British Film Festival held in Dinard in France that celebrates the work of, among others, the British director Mike Leigh, who AS Film Studies students may be familiar with as the director of *Secrets and Lies* (1996, UK/France). Should this lead to a reappraisal of Leigh's work? Can his films be defined in terms of the British context in which they are set or do they better fall into the broader category of World cinema? See **Worksheets 3** and **4**.

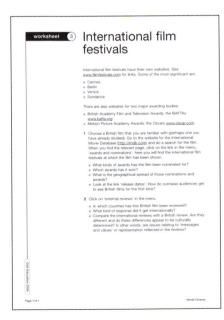

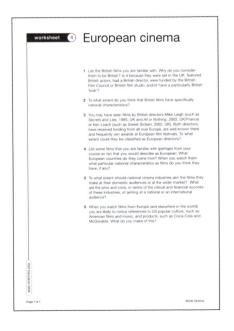

Students should consider:

- Leigh has been nominated for Oscars for *Topsy-Turvy* (1999, UK) and *Secrets and Lies*, as well as winning a number of other US film awards.
- He has also been nominated for awards at the BAFTAs for *Topsy-Turvy*.
- He has won awards for Best Foreign Film in Argentina, Berlin and Cannes.

Other British directors include:

Guy Ritchie, director of *Lock, Stock and Two Smoking Barrels* (1998, UK) and *Snatch* (2000, UK/USA), a British co-production with Hollywood.

- Ritchie was nominated for a BAFTA and various other British awards for *Lock, Stock and Two Smoking Barrels*.
- He was nominated for an award at the Dinard British Film Festival in France, for *Snatch*.
- He won Best Director award for *Lock, Stock and Two Smoking Barrels* at the Tokyo Film Festival.

Danny Boyle, director of *Trainspotting* (1996, UK), *Shallow Grave* (1994, UK) and *The Beach* (2000, USA), another British co-production with Hollywood.

- Boyle was nominated for a BAFTA for best film for *Trainspotting* and won the same award for *Shallow Grave*.
- He was nominated for an award at the Berlin Film Festival for *The Beach*.
- He won an award in Czechoslovakia for *Trainspotting*.
- Boyle won an award at the Dinard Film Festival for *Shallow Grave*.

A further point to consider here is the different definitions of 'British cinema'. Is it possible to unify the countries that constitute the British Isles under this one title? *Trainspotting*, for example, is set in Scotland and based on a book by a Scottish author. The director Danny Boyle is himself Scottish. What added cultural perspective might this give? What if an English director had undertaken the project?

How to use this guide

While the subject of this guide is World cinema, it is impossible to arrive at an understanding of the key issues without focusing on and comparing national cinemas. It is crucial to investigate the national context of any cinema: how historic, cultural, economic and political events influence creative output. In this guide we offer some case studies through which students can reflect on the cultural impact of economic and political events.

- One of the greatest international political events in recent times, the reunification of Hong Kong with China, has inevitably had cultural repercussions, including a considerable impact on the cinema of these two countries.

- We are also seeing a re-emergence of Scandinavian cinema, specifically the current 'export value' of films by Lars von Trier and Thomas Vinterberg from Denmark, and Lukas Moodysson from Sweden.
- In the past, France has enjoyed a higher profile than other countries when it comes to international cinema, but is currently experiencing a renaissance with the release of controversial films such as *Baise-moi* (Coralie Virginie Despentes, 2000, France) and *La Haine*. *La Haine* and *Beau travail*, the latter a focus film on the A2 Film Studies Specification (from June 2004), are both looked at in some detail in this guide.

The following films are recommended to focus students' thinking about national cinemas and are referred to in some detail in this guide and the worksheets:

Beau travail	Claire Denis	France	1998
Chocolat	Claire Denis	France/West Germany/Cameroon	1988
Chungking Express	Wong Kar-Wai	Hong Kong	1994
Do the Right Thing	Spike Lee	USA	1989
La Haine	Mathieu Kassovitz	France	1995
The Idiots	Lars von Trier	Denmark/Sweden/France/Netherlands/Italy	1998
In the Mood for Love	Wong Kar-Wai	Hong Kong/France/Thailand	2000
Show Me Love	Lukas Moodysson	Sweden	1998

The schemes of work outlined in the following pages offer ways of structuring your approach to teaching this topic. They provide guidelines, but you will need to adapt them to your specific needs. Section 2 provides some background information, outlining approaches to the terms and concepts that students may be familiar with from their previous studies of film or media, but suggesting ways in which students might revisit and reconsider these in the context of studying World cinema. Section 3 provides case studies of the four national cinemas indicated above. Although this models approaches to the study of national cinemas, it is not intended to dictate the cinemas your students should study.

Worksheets have been developed to support the suggestions in this guide. You can access these through the website: www.bfi.org.uk/tfms. Click on the title of this guide then enter the user name: **worldcine** and password: **te2711wo**.

Scheme of Work 1: East Asian Cinema

This unit has been designed to introduce students to concepts relating to World cinema, while at the same time providing them with the opportunity to challenge some of the assumptions they may have. Class exercises are designed to enable students to compare and contrast mainstream cinema with more challenging material.

Similarly, students will be able to identify techniques and form, eg in Hong Kong cinema, which correspond with Western filmmaking techniques. There is potential here for showing crossover films, such as those of John Woo, who has enjoyed success in both Hong Kong and Hollywood.

The Hong Kong films used within this scheme of work provide an opportunity to investigate films that could be said to fall into the Art cinema category (see p22–4), at least by Western definitions. This categorisation is supported by the distribution context of such films in the West, raising issues of audience, exhibition etc.

The scheme of work could act as a template for studying other examples of World cinema. Certainly, a similar approach could be adapted to some extent for the study of cinemas of Central and South America, Africa and India.

Overall, the sessions are designed as an introduction to the topic, while at the same time providing a forum to challenge preconceptions that may be held about such films and the national cinemas, and indeed countries, from which they emerge.

Aims
- To consider whether 'World cinema' is a valid term;
- To explore key concepts as they apply to non-mainstream films from around the world, with principal reference to East Asian cinema.

Outcomes
Students will:
- Develop an appreciation of what cinema has to offer beyond the mainstream films distributed in the UK (Hollywood and British cinema);
- Enhance their grasp of key concepts as a progression from study at AS Level, applying these to a broader range of films;
- Be able to contextualise films in both a national cinema and a broader context.

Week 1 Introduction to World cinema: Case study of Hong Kong

- Brainstorm the term 'World cinema', comparing it to the term 'World music'
  (Worksheet 1)

- In pairs: Draw up a list of films set (partly or entirely) in China and Hong Kong. Consider why Hollywood films dominate this list and how these films represent China and Hong Kong

- Recommended extract screening 1: Hong Kong action films directed by John Woo, for example: *A Better Tomorrow* (1986), *Bullet in the Head* (1990), *Hard-Boiled* (1992), *The Killer* (1989)

- Recommended extract screening 2: Hollywood action films, also directed by John Woo, for example: *Broken Arrow* (1996), *Face/Off* (1997), *Mission: Impossible II* (2000)

- Discussion: What differences/similarities are there in terms of one director working within two different film systems? Hong Kong has been described as 'the Hollywood of the East'. Do the clips support this view?
  This will raise issues concerning the purpose of the films as well as their cultural and social context

- Consider Hong Kong cinema as rated by critics, focusing on the critical response to *Chungking Express*
  (Worksheet 7)

Week 2 Experiencing World cinema: The Far East as 'other'

- Make connections between Hong Kong cinema as a New Wave and as Art cinema
  (Worksheet 6)

- Class activity: Extract analysis of *Chungking Express*
  (Worksheet 9)

- Compare this with an opening sequence of a film directed by John Woo to highlight the different approaches, in relation to a different target audience

- Recommended screening 1: *Chungking Express*

- Class activity: Recast the four principal characters in *Chungking Express* using Hollywood actors. Does this change the message or meaning of the film? Would the film now have a wider appeal than the Art cinema audience?
  (Worksheet 2)

Week 3 World cinema as distinct from Western cinema? Culture and history

- Explain some of the social, cultural or historical background of the focus films (See Bibliography for recommended reading.)

- Read and discuss extracts from newspaper/magazine articles in relation to the focus films, eg What have we seen in our films that reflect the situation outlined in this article? Suggested resource: articles by Tony Rayns in *Sight and Sound* magazine (Bibliography, pp82–3)

- Reconsideration of *Chungking Express* as a film reflecting a period of uncertainty and change

Week 4 World cinema as distinct from Western cinema? *Auteurism*

- The director as *auteur*

- Extracts from interviews and profiles of chosen director from DVD extra features: eg The interview with the director on the *In the Mood for Love* special edition

- Activity: Internet research on Wong Kar-Wai – official website and fan websites. Could also include www.sensesofcinema.com

- What critical commentary exists on this director and how does it help us understand his films?
  (Worksheet 5)

- Recommended screening 2: *In the Mood for Love* Discuss how this film contrasts with *Chungking Express*

Week 5 World cinema as distinct from Western cinema? Funding and distribution

- Activity: Internet research as to how focus film was financed (http://imdb.com). Also find out about its distribution: How many screens showed the film relative to its box-office takings? How many prints were available compared to a Hollywood release?

- Compare this with the funding and distribution of a recent mainstream Hollywood or British film, again considering the number of screens/prints relative to box-office takings

Week 6 World cinema as distinct from Western cinema? Exhibition and distribution

- Recommended extract 1: Opening sequence from *In the Mood for Love*

- Discussion: Does the film have an intended audience?
  To what extent is the audience limited by the distributors, rather than by the film itself? Look at a director's career (eg Wong Kar-Wai) and consider why his later films may attract increased funding and distribution, and what difference this makes

- Activity: Plan a Far East film season. Where would the films be shown? Who would the target audience be? What features do they share that would enable you to sell them as a collection? What would be their USP (unique selling point)?

- Activity: Visit a venue (or its website) where such films are shown, often in seasons profiling a director or a particular moment in film history, eg the National Film Theatre in London; The Watershed in Bristol; The Cornerhouse in Manchester

- Activity: The use of international film festivals to promote World cinema.
  (Worksheet 3)

Week 7 Making connections: World cinema and Western cinema

- Discussion: How does *Chungking Express* as an East Asian film reference Western youth culture?

- Consider:
  Wong Kar-Wai's use of the same stylist and cinematographer in his films: Why does he do this? How does this affect his *auteur* status?

  The success of his films beyond East Asia and the impact this has on his subsequent films
  (Worksheet 8)

Schemes of Work 2 and 3: European Cinema

These schemes of work are designed to introduce students to aspects of European cinema, using the case studies of France, Sweden and Denmark. As with Scheme of Work 1, there is potential here to extend beyond these three national cinemas through the application of key concepts to other European countries.

The schemes of work are designed to challenge the validity of terms such as 'World cinema'. Students may come to the conclusion that, through the process of classification (by using terms such as 'World cinema' and 'European cinema'), we may be sectioning off and indeed closing down certain types of national cinema. Added to this is a tendency to place our own nation outside these classifications. To what extent is British cinema European cinema?

This topic will give students the opportunity to engage in highly relevant and contentious debates about national identity, including how they define their own. (See p25 for some introductory comments.) Indeed a useful starting point would be to consider:

- How national identity is constructed and represented by a variety of factors, not least the creative output of a particular country;
- How and why generalisations and national stereotypes have been constructed;
- How these might influence our responses to the films of different countries and cultures, as well as our own.

Again, starting with students' own experience and identity is important. For example, you could do this by looking at the specific issue of the cultural influences of the USA on Britain, whether in popular music, fashion or colloquial language, as well as in film and television and other aspects of popular culture.

Arguably, all international film is inevitably compared, by various criteria, to the output of Hollywood, and is frequently economically affected by it, whether in production, distribution or exhibition. So it is hard to ignore the background role of Hollywood in the study of World cinema, not least because it is likely to be the source of your students' preconceptions about it.

It should also be borne in mind, however, despite the long migration of talent from other cinemas to Hollywood, that the traffic is occasionally two-way. Students may find it interesting to investigate the origins of many a Hollywood mainstream hit, derived from a European original, such as *Vanilla Sky* (Cameron Crowe, 2001, USA) or *The Assassin* (John Badham, 1993, USA).

As with Scheme of work 1, the sessions should provide a basis with which to challenge assumptions and preconceptions about national cinemas.

Aims

- To introduce and investigate key concepts, as they apply to the term World cinema and indeed, European cinema;
- To explore how these films might be placed as World cinema or European cinema;
- To consider the British context and the extent to which it can be understood as part of World cinema.

Outcomes

Students will:

- Have an appreciation of what cinema has to offer beyond the mainstream films distributed in the UK;
- Have further insight into key concepts and how they apply to a wider range of films;
- Be able to place films within a national cinema as well as a broader context, for example, European cinema.

● Scheme of work 2: European cinema: France

Week 1 British Cinema as European Cinema

- Recommended extract 1: From films by Mike Leigh as a British director achieving recognition and attracting funding from Europe: *Secrets and Lies*, *All or Nothing* (2002, UK/France)

- Recommended extract 2: From films by Ken Loach, who similarly enjoys success in Europe, sometimes filming on location outside Britain: *Land and Freedom* (1995, UK/Spain/Germany/Italy), *Bread and Roses* (2000, UK/Germany/Spain/France/Italy/ Switzerland) **(Worksheet 4)**

Week 2 France as a national cinema

- Discussion: What awareness do students have of diversity within European cinema? Does the term apply to British cinema? **(Worksheet 4)**

- Recommended extracts: Opening sequences of contemporary films with French connections, reflecting different genres: *Amélie* (Jean-Pierre Jeunet, 2001, France/Germany), *La Haine*, *Code Unknown* (Michael Haneke, 2000, France/Germany/Romania), *Harry He's Here to Help* (Dominik Moll, 2000, France), *Chocolat* (Lasse Halleström, 2000, UK/USA) set in France, but funded with US money

- What characterises these films as French? Are they all equally 'French'?

Week 3 France as European cinema

- Recommended screening 1: *La Haine*

- Discussion: Could *La Haine* have been set in Britain or the USA? If so, who would star in it and who would direct it? What added perspective does this give to the film's classification as French or European?

- Recommended extract 1: Opening sequence of *La Haine*

- Recommended extract 2: If possible, compare with closing sequence (riot scene) of *Do the Right Thing* (Spike Lee, 1989, USA) – a screening of the whole film would be useful as an example of a US independent film tackling similar themes

- Activity: What similarities/differences can be drawn between the two films? Consider the films' textual features, as well as where they were made

Week 4 Representations of France

- Activity: Research contextual background to *La Haine* of rioting in the *banlieue* (suburbs) of Paris since the 1980s: see 'After the Riot', *Sight and Sound*, November 1995

- Recommended extract 1: Hollywood representations of France: Could include some or all of *Forget Paris* (Billy Crystal, 1995, USA), *French Kiss* (Lawrence Kasdan, 1995, USA/UK), *Everyone Says I Love You* (Woody Allen, 1996, USA)

- Recommended extract 2: Some or all of, eg, *Les Nuits fauves* (Cyril Collard, 1992, France/Italy), *Beau travail*

- Contrast how these films and *La Haine* represent France with the way the country is represented in Hollywood films

Week 5 The *auteur* within French cinema

- Activity: Compare the directors of French films studied so far: Can similarities and/or differences be identified? Can these be compared to the work of British directors?

- Approaches to close study films: the director as *auteur* **(Worksheet 15)**

Week 6 French cinema as art cinema: Stylistic features

- Recommended screening: *Beau travail*

- Consideration of *Beau travail* as example of art cinema, directed by a female *auteur*
(Worksheet 16)

Week 7 French cinema as Art cinema: Distribution context

- Activity: Trace the box-office performance of *Beau travail* in the UK and the USA **(Worksheet 17)**

- Activity: Plan a season of films on French cinema that includes the ones within this section **(Worksheet 18)**

- ## Scheme of work 3: Denmark and Sweden

Week 1 The revival of the Danish film industry

- Consideration of a national cinema enjoying a revival
Do the films contain characteristics of New Wave cinema?
(**Worksheet 6**)

- Recommended extracts 1: Two or three of the following from Denmark: *Festen*, *The Idiots*, *Mifune* (Søren Kragh-Jacobsen, 1999, Denmark/Sweden), *Italian for Beginners* (Lone Scherfig, 2000, Denmark/Sweden)

Week 2 Denmark as an emerging cinema

- Production context of *Festen*: 'micro' studio reflecting 'macro' circumstances of the Danish film industry
(Worksheet 13)

- Recommended screening 1: *Festen*

Week 3 Art cinema as shocking cinema

- Use *The Idiots* as a case study example of film censorship in the UK – it can be considered also as an example of shocking cinema, alongside *Festen*
(Worksheet 14)

- Recommended screening 2: *The Idiots*

Week 4 The Dogme 95 manifesto and its contribution to Art cinema

- Activity: How do the form and style of *The Idiots* contribute to its impact?
  (Worksheet 12)

Week 5 Contemporary Swedish cinema

- Recommended extracts: Three by Swedish director Lukas Moodysson: *Show Me Love*, *Together* (2000, Sweden/Denmark/ Italy), *Lilya 4-Ever* (2002, Sweden/Denmark)

Week 6 The revival of the Swedish film industry

- Explore the contextual background *Show Me Love* (**Worksheet 10**)

- Recommended screening 3: *Show Me Love*

Week 7 Style and form of Swedish cinema

- Messages and values within *Show Me Love* (**Worksheet 11**)

Background information

The study of World cinema requires a critical application of the key concepts of Film and Media Studies, exposing these concepts to question in relation to films from a broad range of national cinemas. It is important to encourage students to question their assumptions about foreign-language films. You may well have students with an established interest in and receptiveness to such films, but even enthusiasts need to be aware of the wider contexts in which these films can be examined.

At the same time, the intention is not to limit students' experience of the films by channelling them into particular ways of thinking or by providing formulaic answers to exam topics or coursework. Rather, the intention is to encourage students to discover films with which they were previously unfamiliar so that they can develop their own interest in different national cinemas. In the short term, we have in mind the requirements of coursework and exams. Ultimately, however, we would hope students develop an interest in a wide range of films.

It is also worth encouraging students to consider the impact that other cinemas have had on Hollywood production. Hollywood films have consistently adopted ideas and techniques from European cinema and cross-fertilisation has existed throughout the history of cinema. For example, the German director F W Murnau, working in both the German and Hollywood studio systems in the 1920s, pioneered the use of Expressionistic lighting to create certain effects. Thus, the film *Sunrise* made by Murnau for the Fox Film Corporation in the USA in 1927 can be said to be as much a German Expressionist film as *Nosferatu*, which was made for the UFA studio in Germany in 1922.

It should also be borne in mind, particularly with reference to the features discussed below, that there is no such thing as a typical World cinema film. The term is a collective one for all manner of films from different national cinemas and cannot adequately label a single type. In addition, it should not be assumed that all examples of World cinema are necessarily Art or alternative cinema, as a mainstream national cinema clearly exists in most countries. However, it tends to be only art-house films from other countries that are distributed internationally, typically following film festivals. A look at Australian or French commercial film sites, for example, will show many popular and successful titles that never reach the UK.

Below are some key terms and concepts which form the basis of study around World cinema.

Categories of cinema

- ## Art cinema

The writers Susan Hayward and Geoffrey Nowell-Smith both make a significant contribution to an understanding of the idea of Art cinema. Susan Hayward, a specialist on French cinema, describes Art cinema as

> a certain type of European cinema that is experimental in technique and narrative. This cinema, which typically produces low- to mid-budget films, attempts to address the aesthetics of cinema and cinematic practices and is primarily, but not exclusively, produced outside dominant cinema systems. (1997, p8).

- Hayward here confines the definition of Art cinemas to European and American underground films. Students could consider whether the films they are studying can be defined in Hayward's terms. To what extent do the examples suggested in this guide fit into this definition? *Beau travail*, *Show Me Love* and *The Idiots* could all fit this definition.
- Could it equally apply to non-European films such as *Chungking Express* and *In the Mood for Love*?
- Is it appropriate to describe Hong Kong cinema as not having a dominant cinema system?

Hayward goes on to discuss narrative in Art cinema:

> Generally speaking, in art cinema narrative codes and conventions are disturbed, the narrative line is fragmented so there is no seamless cause and effect storyline. Similarly, characters' behaviour appears contingent, hesitant rather than assured and 'in the know' or motivated towards certain ambitions, goals or desires. Although these films are character, rather than plot-led, there are no heroes; in fact this absence of heroes is an important feature of art cinema. (1997, p10)

Again, this approach can be discussed after viewing the films. Students may feel that rather than the films lacking a central hero, there is instead a lack of a star, albeit that the actors may well be stars in their own countries.

Hayward makes a further point:

> This [Art] cinema, in its rupture with classic narrative cinema, intentionally distances spectators to create a reflective space for them to assume their own critical space or subjectivity in relation to the screen or film. (1997, p10)

You could discuss with your students:

- Do they feel more distanced from the films they are studying than from the films they watch for entertainment? Are they at the same time more empowered in their interpretations?
- Is the opposite true when viewing more mainstream Hollywood films or are these texts also open to a multiple range of viewpoints?

These questions are developed in the section on Spectatorship (see p29).

Geoffrey Nowell-Smith offers a different approach to Art cinema. In a discussion of the economic rise and fall of European cinema during the 1950s and 1960s, he discusses the perception of Art cinema as films at the low- and mid-budget levels, while those with higher budgets are seen as 'international film'. But, as he points out, this can be misleading when considering European films from certain periods:

> Many films marketed in Britain and America under the art cinema label, and imagined to be somehow different from 'commercial' films were in fact (and sometimes still are) mainstream products in their country of origin, enjoying popular success at home before being sold abroad for more restricted 'art-house' release. (1997)

Nowell-Smith emphasises the need for differentiation; that it is not possible to place the term 'Art cinema' on all cinemas of Europe at any one time. Taking examples from an earlier period, he suggests that Art cinema could include both low-budget films of the French New Wave of the late 1950s and early 1960s, and high-budget films such as the Italian film *The Leopard* (Luchino Visconti, 1963, Italy/France), actually funded by Twentieth-Century Fox.

However, these various strands of Art cinema share common ground in that the commercial success or otherwise of these films is dependent on factors which are generally different to more mainstream films. As Nowell-Smith points out, Art cinema relies more on showcase opportunities, such as international film festivals, including Cannes, Venice and Berlin. The recognition a film receives at a festival depends on its critical reception; this increases its chances of getting a distribution contract. In commercial terms, it is at this point that Art cinema can become mainstream cinema. The critical acclaim received by *Chungking Express*, for example, led to it having more widespread distribution, and therefore commercial success, in both the art-house and mainstream arenas.

Students will know that almost every newly released film has a website. They may be less familiar with film festival websites that can provide useful information about a film's target audience. They may find that some of these websites present British cinema on the world stage, often enjoying greater recognition in countries other than the UK. For more on the function of film festivals, see **Worksheet 3**.

● European cinema

Can the varying cinematic forms emerging from diverse European countries be collectively termed European cinema? Again, it's a question of perspective. Susan Hayward argues that:

> Viewed from the United States, particularly Hollywood, European cinema since the 1920s has been construed as a global concept and perceived as meaning two distinct things. First, European cinema is predominantly 'art cinema' … second it is the only true rival to Hollywood and must at all costs be infiltrated and dominated. (1997, p89)

Hayward describes Hollywood as being 'the point of reference. Thus in Western Europe a nation's cinema is defined, in part, in relation to what it is not (that is, "not Hollywood") in relation to an "other".' (1997, p90). Hayward also points out that, in the 1980s, both Britain and France enjoyed success in the USA with post-heritage films such as *Manon des Sources* (Claude Berri, 1986, France/Italy/Switzerland), *Cyrano de Bergerac* (Jean-Paul Rappeneau, 1990, France), *A Room with a View* (James Ivory, 1985, UK) and *Howards End* (James Ivory, 1991, UK/Japan). This success continued into the 1990s with more diverse films of a particularly British flavour such as *Trainspotting* and *The Full Monty* (Peter Cattaneo, 1997, UK), the latter attracting distribution money from Twentieth-Century Fox.

The classification of European cinema has been reappraised during the 1990s, following an increase in academic study, which has linked national cinemas with national identity and examined the role played by the European Union in promoting the film industries of Europe. As Ginette Vincendeau points out, 'there is a tension between a search for common features – "the European" – and a desire to isolate or preserve national specificity' (1998, p447).

After showing a few European films you could ask students to respond to the following:

- To what extent do they feel that their close study films fit into the category of European cinema?
- Do the European films featured in this resource fit into this definition?
- Do they have a sense of Europe being a rival to Hollywood? (This is a good way in to a study of distribution, exhibition etc.)
- Where does British cinema fit? Is it a rival of either Hollywood or European (ie foreign-language) films?

Courtesy of *bfi* Stills

Festen

● National cinemas

The approach taken in this guide is to offer implicit or explicit comparisons between national cinemas and Hollywood. For this reason, it is perhaps difficult to consider the USA as a national cinema in its own right, as its pervasiveness in the West is almost regarded as a given. As Stephen Crofts puts it:

> Western nation-state cinemas are habitually defined against Hollywood. It is hardly ever spoken of as a national cinema, perhaps because of its transnational reach. This has been further consolidated since the 1980s by its increased domination of West European screens and the substantial inroads it has made into East European and other new markets. (1998, p390)

By contrast, however, the level of commercial success enjoyed by films from the Asian continent means that 'Indian and Hong Kong cinemas can afford to ignore Hollywood, while Japanese production sometimes outstrips Hollywood imports at the local box office.' (Lent 1990, p47)

It is also worth considering that the films we see here from other national cinemas may not be representative of what is popular in their countries of origin. Ironically, it is the more popular films within a nation's output that may be more demanding, and therefore less attractive, for many British audiences, in terms of the need to interpret the cultural codes embedded within the text that make a film work for its national audience. The more frequently exported art-house cinema release tends to assume an audience educated in European or American traditions of filmmaking.

With these points in mind, students could consider the future of national cinemas in the light of an increasing number of international co-productions, as well as new technologies that threaten to break down the barriers of physical distance, especially in terms of digital exhibition at cinemas and on television worldwide, not least with the rise of cable TV. It is worth noting that many of the case study and focus films have funding from more than one country. How does this affect their definition as cultural expressions of either a national cinema, World cinema or a new form of international cinema?

● Cinematic New Waves

'New Wave' is a term generally used to describe a group of films emerging at certain times out of specific cultural and historical contexts. Two of the most prominent of these are the French New Wave, which arose in Paris in the late 1950s, and the Hong Kong New Wave, emerging at the time of Hong Kong's reunification with China.

New Wave films are categorised as having a distinctive style, ideology or attitude – in the case of the French New Wave, the use of hand-held cameras enabled directors to apparently film the here and now on the streets of Paris, giving their films a more carefree style. The directors of the French New Wave were well versed in film theory and criticism, and experimented with notions of film realism, how a film should look and could be made. This is a major factor in its influence of subsequent cinema. New Wave cinemas can stretch the boundaries of filmmaking, with low-budget films conveying an exuberance and freedom lacking in more mainstream films. Often such New Waves can help to revitalise the mainstream film industries.

The term 'New Wave' has been used to describe some British films of the late 1950s and early 1960s. These films featured younger directors and casts. Many of the films were adapted from books written by emerging playwrights, focusing on young people and addressing, in social realist style, issues such as underage pregnancy, single parenthood, mixed-race relationships, juvenile delinquency and so on.

A further example is Dogme 95: a collection of films which has been described as being part of a Danish New Wave because they challenged the conventions of mainstream cinema by establishing their own set of 'anti-rules'. None of the techniques used is especially new, but they signify a return to a simpler style, one which students may feel complements the messages and values inscribed within the film text.

Courtesy of *bfi* Stills

The Idiots

More recently, a New Wave in Mexican and Latin American, sometimes called Chicano, cinema has emerged, with *Central Station* (Walter Salles, 1998, Brazil/France), *Behind the Sun* (Walter Salles, 2001, Brazil/France/Switzerland), *City of God* (Kátia Lund and Fernando Meirelles, 2002, Brazil/France/USA), *Y Tu Mamá También* (Alfonso Curaón, 2001, USA/Mexico) and *Amores Perros* (Alejandro González Iñárritu, 2000, Mexico) and *21 Grams* (Alejandro González Iñárritu, 2003, Mexico). Incidentally, most of these directors have gone on to work on Hollywood projects.

Students may wish to approach New Waves in the following ways:

● Examples of cinematic New Waves from Hong Kong (*Chungking Express*) and Denmark (*The Idiots*) are contained in this guide. Could the term also be applied to Sweden (*Show Me Love*)?

- After viewing extracts from any of the case study films, students could consider what constitutes a New Wave in terms of look, style and theme.
- Students could explore the historical and social contexts of the films, as these are inextricably linked with their New Wave classification.
- They could make connections between the internal features of a film text and the context in which it is made. (Film Studies at A2 Level requires this.)

Key terms and concepts

● Audience

Audience as a concept tends to have a different emphasis in Media Studies and Film Studies. Broadly speaking, the Media Studies approach is concerned with reception, ie how audiences are positioned by media texts and targeted by media producers, which are nevertheless subject to multiple readings by the spectator (see Spectatorship). The Film Studies approach includes elements of this, plus a consideration of the actual location of consumption, ie the kinds of venues that may exhibit international films, together with the spectator's individual response to the film.

A consideration of the concept of audience involves an understanding of viewers as constituting a number of different groups, rather than one collective group consuming a film text in the same way. For example, consider the audience for a Chinese or Indian film in their own continents, compared to the audience for such films in this country.

- Who are the films aimed at in this country?
- How are UK audiences likely to respond to the very different style and intention of a Chinese or Indian film?

If possible, show extracts to students from a Bollywood film (see the BFI Teaching Guide *Bollywood and Beyond*, or you may catch an Indian film showing late at night on Channel 4). Ask them to consider the cultural messages and values implicit in the text.

- What significance does music and dance have in the narrative?
- What do these suggest to us about gender or family relationships?
- What cultural function do the stars appear to have?

We may consider the audiences in terms of the marketing strategies designed to target them. For example,

- Who are the audiences for foreign-language films and how does this impact on where they are shown? Would it be more appropriate to address the question the other way around?

- Is the place of exhibition the main factor in determining who will see foreign-language films?
- Get students to consider themselves as an audience:
  - Ask them to collect listings information from their local newspaper. If possible, this should be from a multiplex as well as from a smaller independent venue, eg The Cornerhouse in Manchester, The Duke of York's in Brighton, The Chapterhouse in Cardiff, Watershed in Bristol.
  - If there are only multiplexes or large cinema chains in your neighbourhood (this in itself raises certain issues), ask students to check out the alternatives via their websites.
  - If you live in a city that has its own listing magazine (for example, *Time Out* in London) or if there is something similar in your local paper, these can be brought to class also.
  - Discuss with students what films they were already aware of and whether there were any lower profile films in their material.
  - What kinds of film are extensively offered by the multiplexes? Are there any films other than Hollywood high-concept films or heavily marketed British films?
  - Would they and their friends spontaneously consider going to see a foreign-language and/or a British Art film? What factors would encourage or discourage them from doing this?

● Spectatorship

Students are used to watching films as a leisure activity, but studying World cinema offers opportunities to interpret and appreciate a wider variety of film texts in a different way. To begin with students might find non-Hollywood mainstream films difficult to follow, with their lack of familiar narrative and genre codes, which usually guide viewers through the act of looking. However, watching very different films may enable them to reconsider how they view films and their relationship with these films as spectators. In particular, they need to keep in mind that, in all likelihood, they are not the intended audience for the film. How does this affect their ability to read the film? What is the filmmaker presuming about the way the audience will read the film?

Laura Mulvey's influential article 'Visual Pleasure and Narrative Cinema' (1975), about spectatorship, focused on the relationship between the film text and the male viewer. It examined the privileging of the male gaze in relation to the female form on screen, focusing on classic Hollywood feature films. However, Mulvey and others reconsidered this theory in subsequent years, arguing that an understanding of spectatorship must take into account not only the gender, but also the class, race or cultural expectations of the viewer, which contribute to his or her reading of a text.

The case study on *Beau travail* provides a framework with which to challenge and explore spectatorship (see pp70–74).

Students should be encouraged to think about the following when considering spectatorship in relation to World cinema:

- How are we being positioned by the film text, bearing in mind that we were probably not the intended target audience initially?
- Does the director have a particular intention or message to convey, beyond the need to entertain?
- To what extent are the target audience repositioned by the film text?

● Industry/Institution

This key concept refers to the production, distribution and exhibition of a film, and students could consider a variety of aspects when studying World cinema:

- The evolution and history of a national cinema;
- The source(s) of film finance and arrangements such as co-productions with other countries;
- The ownership of film production, distribution and exhibition companies;
- The effects of globalisation;
- Whether the film is produced within a mainstream industry or is independent;
- The effect a film's institutional context has on its content and reception;
- How film genre and the status of the director relate to film marketing and audiences;
- How casting choices and star status relate to film marketing and audiences;
- How international film festivals and awards play an important role in film production, distribution and exhibition;
- The degree of influence on a film director's treatment of his/her subject matter by film producers;
- The role of state in relation to film production, distribution and exhibition;
- Censorship and certification;
- The role of Hollywood in relation to national cinemas.

The case studies offer accounts of the institutional contexts of the national cinemas featured here teachers can model their own case studies on.

● Representation (or messages and values)

The worksheets that accompany this resource are designed to raise questions about how cultures are represented, literally *re*-presented to us, on screen and by whom. While national identity is an obvious consideration in a study of World cinema, it would also be appropriate to look at the configuration of gender relationships in the film. For instance, French director Claire Denis has admitted that she likes 'writing stories about men not because I want to dominate them but because I like to observe and imagine them. A man is a different world and this masculinity interests me.' (Darke, 2000, p.17). Students could consider this quote when watching the scenes from *Beau travail* suggested in **Worksheet 16**.

The concepts of representation and ideology, in World cinema, involve issues which students can examine, in relation to their focus or chosen films. For example:

- Cultural imperialism
- Dominant, subordinate and radical ideology
- Ethnocentricity
- Globalisation
- Hegemony
- Post-colonialism
- Religion
- Sexuality
- Race
- Politics

The case studies explore several of these issues in reference to specific films featured here.

(For an overview of this key concept, see the *bfi* pack on *Representation* by Roy Stafford.)

● Critical theory and how to use it

Lengthy handouts on critical theory should be avoided, as this is likely to be inaccessible to most students; instead, brief quotations from academic sources can be used to confirm or challenge ideas about a particular film or national cinema. See **Worksheet 5** for an example of this using *Chungking Express*. You could use the academic references in this guide with students to stimulate discussion and deeper study. It is important to understand that the purpose of using critical theory or critical perspectives with students is to extend their personal response to a film text, by introducing them to ideas they may not have initially considered.

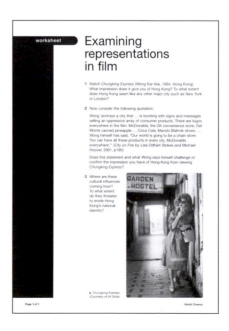

31

Critical theory is not an end in itself, and examiners are rarely impressed by name-dropping which demonstrates little understanding of how an idea has been applied. The meaningful application of theory, to specific examples from the text itself, is to be encouraged. At A Level, however, this is secondary to the student's primary study of the text. Students must attribute all quotes and major ideas/concepts, in keeping with academic conventions.

● Film grammar and style

A study of World cinema enables students to rethink concepts familiar from their study at AS Level, including genre, narrative and film style. For example,

- To what extent is our understanding of genre useful in classifying our two case study films from Hong Kong?
- Similarly, do we have to rethink our ideas of narrative when viewing films that appear to be episodic in nature, rather than strictly motivated by cause and effect, such as Bollywood films?

On its release in the UK in 1995, *Chungking Express* was described in *Sight and Sound* by Tony Rayns as:

> … a director's film. The level of invention in the plotting and the film language is almost profligate and the wit of the writing leaves the average Tarantino dialogue sounding like sitcom filler. (1995, p48)

Chungking Express

Courtesy of *bfi Stills*

Students may feel that the techniques used in Hong Kong films are far more overt than they are in most Hollywood films. In the case of *Chungking Express*, the film draws attention to itself through the use of jump cuts, hand-held camera and stop-motion photography. Contrast this with *In the Mood for Love* which has greater emphasis on mood created by lighting, with less obvious use of visual devices. (Approaches to textual analysis of *Chungking Express* are contained in **Worksheet 9**.)

● Textual analysis

Media and Film specifications at A2 Level require that students have an in-depth knowledge of their chosen or focus film. This should reflect the film's production and audience context, as well as its textual properties. It is to the students' advantage to use appropriate terminology when analysing their films, as examiners are looking for an eye for detail, and an understanding of these terms with reference to the text as evidence to reinforce a point, rather than straightforward description.

Short extract analysis using the opening/ending sequence or pivotal turning point within a film, for example, can provide students with a basis for exploring different key concepts, such as messages and values in Film Studies or representation in Media Studies.

Deconstruction of film texts at A2 Level often builds on that which has been covered at AS Level. A good approach is to revise these concepts by first showing a short clip from your close study film, followed by some diagnostic questioning to allow students to recap key film terms.

You can take this a stage further by posing questions such as:

- Does the film clearly fit into a particular genre, in the way we have come to understand it?
- Does it have a conventional narrative and does the opening sequence follow a similar establishing pattern to mainstream films?
- What do you think the director is trying to do here? (This encourages students to offer a more objective personal response.)
- What are the messages and values/representational issues conveyed through this extract and how effective are the cinematic devices used to show them? (This encompasses the kind of approach required at A2 Film Studies.)

For a full exploration of film language and further advice as to how to analyse films, see *Teaching Analysis of Film Language and Production* by Elaine Scarratt, in the same *bfi* series.

● Key terms for textual analysis

Cinematography

In his book *The Language of Cinema*, Kevin Jackson offers this definition of the work of the cinematographer as:

> … the person in charge (generally after consultation with the director) of lighting the set and actors; setting up and moving the camera; selecting appropriate lenses, stocks, filters; establishing the composition of images and so on; in general, then, the person who helps create what can loosely be called the 'look' of a film, its visual identity. (1998, p48).

This definition clearly affects the concept of 'authorship' (see pp38–41). Those students who have chosen to study an auteur's film can approach this in terms of the relationship the *auteur* shares with a key partner – often a cinematographer, editor or producer. For example, fans of Martin Scorsese may be unaware of his long-term collaboration with his editor, Thelma Schoonmaker, and the contribution she makes to his *auteur* signature, through developing a distinctive style and look. Similarly, the tensions present in Alfred Hitchcock's working relationship with producer David O. Selznick while working in Hollywood had a marked effect on the outcome of his films and, by extension, his *auteur* status.

(See also Sally Potter's comments on 'authorship' in the bfi 16+ study guide on *Auteur Theory/Auteurs*: www.bfi.org.uk/nationallibrary/collections/16+/).

To develop this topic, consider the questions on **Worksheet 6**.

Editing

By controlling time and space within the film narrative, editing plays a central role in constructing the film in its final form, controlling time and space within film narrative. Continuity editing often creates the illusion of a seamless transition over time and locations. Editing enables scenes to be constructed so that they make sense to the viewer. It can also control the positioning of the viewer in relation to the characters through, for example, point-of-view shots.

More experimental forms of editing have been linked with Art cinema (pp22–4). For example, an Art film may employ an editing style that disorients the viewer, subverting the process of 'becoming lost' in the narrative by interrupting conventional narrative flow. While continuity editing makes the construction of the film invisible, allowing the viewer to focus on the narrative, some filmmakers may choose to draw attention to the film as a constructed text, consciously highlighting the editing process through style and technique.

This kind of editing is a trademark of New Wave films, although experiments with editing date back to the earliest days of filmmaking. The Russian director, Sergei Eisenstein, famously experimented with editing in his films, including *The Battleship Potemkin* (1925, Russia), to create a special effect and to enhance the impact of key sequences, notably the Odessa Steps montage sequence. In this example, the jarring effect of jump cuts and the juxtaposition of shots contribute to the creation of meaning in the film – drawing sharp attention to the subject matter.

Increasingly, mainstream films have employed a more obviously constructed style of editing, with the use of dissolves and jump cuts becoming acceptable devices to manipulate time and space.

- Cross-cutting: Students will be familiar with this as a means of creating a sense of the narrative event 'meanwhile' in a film. It is usually apparent that this is happening and easy for us to make that connection in our minds. Yet in the case of *Chungking Express*, the cross-cutting at the beginning of the film gives us little sense of a connection between the characters and events that we see. This seems to act as a metaphor for the lives of the characters within the narrative and enables us to interpret the film quite differently in subsequent viewings. (**See Worksheet 9**)

- Jump cuts: An intentionally visible form of editing used as a stylistic device, the jump cut can be compared with the use of continuity editing as a narrative device. It was most famously used in Jean-Luc Godard's *À Bout de souffle* (1960, France) and is a common feature of New Wave films, as well as music videos. Rather than disorientating the viewer, it is now almost a convention, in the sense that it epitomises New Wave films.

Sound

There are two basic elements to sound on screen:

- **Diegetic sound** emanates from within the world of the film. This may include 'visible' sound such as the dialogue between characters. Sound which is not 'seen' but nevertheless belongs within the frame, such as off-screen footsteps, or a radio playing within the scene, is also considered diegetic.
- **Non-diegetic sound** is added post-production, such as a soundtrack or a voiceover.

An approach to studying sound is to select an extract from your close study film and treat it as a silent film. First show the extract with the sound turned down. What expressive devices are now being revealed, in the absence of sound? Students will be more aware of editing, cinematography and other aspects of form, as well as the way in which soundtracks often act as a narrative device (as in the anti-police song in Mathieu Kassovitz's *La Haine*). Students can then speculate about the appropriate use of sound in the extract. (Something that all of the diverse case study films in this resource share is their use of British and American popular songs, often to signpost a recurring theme and to connect with contemporary audiences.)

A further approach is to consider the sound as discrete from the extract. Listen to an extract with a notable use of sound, without the picture. Do the students think that the music on the soundtrack has been composed for the film or is it an appropriate use of an existing recording? Does it evoke a particular time or place? Is it Anglo-American music (as in the case of *Chungking Express* and *La Haine*)? What expectations does this set up? Assess the significance of the lyrics – are they a direct commentary on the film's narrative or a counterpoint to it?

Mise en scène

To start with you could review what students understand by *mise en scène* by getting them to identify the various elements that comprise a scene in an early sequence of one of the case study or focus films:

- Lighting
- Setting and props
- Positioning of actors/characters and objects
- Facial expressions and body language
- Costume, hair and make-up

Mise en scène is often a defining trademark of a director, but students could consider that in fact *mise en scène* is the result of the contribution by a number of people in addition to the director: the art director, set designer, costume designer, lighting director, editor, etc. In *Chungking Express*, the New Wave look is largely attributed to its director, but how have others contributed to it, eg the cinematographer, Christopher Doyle, and set designer, William Chang? Despite these contributions, how does *mise en scène* remain a defining feature of Wong Kar-Wai's directorial style.

Courtesy of *bfi* Stills

Beau travail

● Genre

Students of A2 Film and Media will be familiar with genre analysis from their studies at AS Level, not least the film industry's dependence on genre recognition as a marketing device for mainstream films. Study of World cinema allows for a reappraisal of genre.

If students were asked to classify their close study films by genre, they may have difficulty using the benchmark of Hollywood or mainstream British films. This is in part due to the nature of the foreign-language films included in the various exam specifications (dictated by what is distributed in the UK), which tend to belong in the Art cinema category (see pp22–4), rather than the more mainstream genre films.

With a focus on European cinema, Ginette Vincendeau describes both genre and stardom as 'the forgotten categories' that have nevertheless always existed in European cinema, albeit that they 'both operate in an unsystematic way compared to Hollywood' (1998, p445). Vincendeau points out some links with Hollywood genres, eg the thriller/film noir genre has been reinvented as the *policier* in postwar French cinema (eg *Bob le flambeur* (1955) and *Le Doulos* (1961), both directed by Jean-Pierre Melville).

Students should be encouraged to consider what genre elements the focus and case study films may feature and to what extent 'genre' remains a useful term in relation to these films.

Narrative analysis

Narrative is concerned with the organisation of space and time in film. What are the codes and conventions or rules used to progress narrative time and space? These include the use of continuity editing and other formal devices. The narrative form of World cinema can be compared to the classic narrative form adopted by mainstream Hollywood films. To what extent do they follow the familiar narrative form (ie the use of continuity editing) and to what extent do they diverge from this?

Like mainstream Hollywood films, World cinema frequently uses binary oppositions as devices to structure the narrative. These tend to focus on oppositions of culture or nationality, gender and race.

Exam specifications relating to Film and Media Studies often link the concepts of narrative and genre. A study of World cinema allows students to question these concepts and their interdependence. The case study films featured here provide a challenge to how we perceive narrative. Both *Chungking Express* and *In the Mood for Love* play around with conventions of time and space, the former utilising the common technique of cross-cutting, but in a way that causes some of the characters' stories to intertwine.

Directors and stars

● *Auteurs*

To introduce the idea of *auteur*, select extracts from one film by a director that you feel marks him or her as being distinctive in some way. You could use one of the directors referred to in this guide: Wong Kar-Wai, Lukas Moodysson, Lars von Trier, Thomas Vinterberg, Claire Denis or Mathieu Kassovitz.

Ask students to suggest whether there are defining moments within these extracts that mark this director as being distinctive. Students should look for consistency in style, themes and approach. Is the director is motivated by the expression of personal vision, rather than necessarily fulfilling the needs of a production company? Comparison with a second film by the same director may help to pin down a certain look, style and theme – this is more likely to be the linking factor, rather than consistency in genre, if indeed their films can be classified in that way. Useful to the analysis of a director's *auteur* status is knowledge of the production circumstances in which a director works. What kind of financial constraints, for example, does the director have to work within? Is he or she in control of any creative or financial aspects of their filmmaking, for example, by writing the screenplay or acting as a producer?

Ideas around authorship can be traced back to the 1920s, but the term was revived most notably in the 1950s through the work of film critics and directors writing for the French film magazine *Cahiers du Cinéma*. Principal among these were André Bazin, Jean-Luc Godard, François Truffaut, Claude Chabrol, Jacques Rivette and Eric Rohmer (who went on to become the directors of the French New Wave).

The editor, André Bazin, was instrumental in analysing the work of directors in new ways and, in particular, he took a distinctive approach to the somewhat underrated directors working in Hollywood within a tightly controlled studio system. Bazin and others praised their work in its own right and by implication, because of the restrictions imposed upon them, said that a directorial 'signature' shone through. For example, Howard Hawks and Nicholas Ray made a wide variety of genre films, but nevertheless, for the *Cahiers* group, an identifiable authorial 'trademark' was evident in their films.

Students are frequently intrigued by the idea of directors as *auteurs*, both as a conceptual theory and in terms of how their personal background informs their work. They are interested in the circumstances that allow *auteurs* a level of artistic freedom and a personal vision to emerge in their films. You could ask them to consider, for example, to what extent Wong Kar-Wai is an *auteur*. His work is sometimes compared to the early films of Jean-Luc Godard, in particular *Chungking Express* with *À Bout de souffle*. Wong Kar-Wai also operates outside the mainstream film system, at the art-house, low-budget end of the market. He was one of the first directors to establish an independent film production company (Jet Tone), an unusual move for a Hong Kong director. One way he sustains his company is by pre-selling his projects in those markets where his name and those of his stars are considered bankable. Another way he retains independence is to make commercials, although this may imply a compromise in terms of his *auteur* status. However Alfred Hitchcock had to work in the Hollywood studio system to gain financial backing, at the cost of more artistic constraint – a compromise from which, many argue, emerged some of his most highly regarded work.

Directors who work independently face the problem of attracting foreign investors who may impose constraints as a condition for backing the film, by insisting on a genre, star and general bankability. They will also wish to see a script. This is difficult in the case of Wong Kar-Wai, as he resists the preparation of detailed scripts in advance of shooting. His method, instead, is to write fairly detailed outlines, retaining the option of deviating from them during production, so the film can grow organically.

This approach may contribute to the look of films such as *Chunking Express*, and yet *In the Mood for Love* has the look of a much more tightly controlled and planned project. Indeed, 'what was envisaged as a low-budget quickie, to be filmed in Hong Kong with two lead actors and a small supporting cast, wound up taking 14 months to script, shoot and edit.' (Tony Rayns, 1996, p14). *Chungking Express*, by contrast, took just three months to make, from shooting to première. Wong Kar-Wai's working method perhaps comes across more strongly in this film; students may consider this unscripted style as an auteurist feature.

Courtesy of *bfi* Stills

In the Mood for Love

A further auteurist feature in Wong Kar-Wai's work is that, although his films appear quite different in terms of content, similarities can be found across them. Tony Rayns (1995) has identified some of these factors as:

- A reluctance to work within a genre format, something that limits a popular audience for his films in Hong Kong. (His box-office performance there has been erratic);
- The casting of indigenous stars against type or in unusual roles (they are apparently very keen to work with him);
- Unpredictability in terms of what the next film may be like; *Chungking Express* was made between *Days of Being Wild* (1991, Hong Kong) and *Ashes of Time* (1994, Hong Kong/China/Taiwan), and yet it would be difficult to place this film alongside the other two;
- Similarities in terms of the themes in his films; all characters experience loneliness, insecurity and the inability to commit (as identified by Wong Kar-Wai himself);
- The ultimate test of an *auteur* – imitation or influence. As Wong Kar-Wai has acknowledged, 'Too many directors are "doing" Wong Kar-Wai these days, so I have to do something different.' (The director in an interview with Tony Rayns, January 2000)

It is important to state here that, despite the compelling and accessible nature of an auteurist approach, it is essential that students understand its problems and limitations and that they are introduced to the key counter arguments and theories. *The Cinema Book*, edited by Pam Cook and Mieke Biernink (*bfi* Publishing, 1999) summarises the history of *auteur* theory and its critiques.

Auteur theory has been subject to periodic reassessment since the 1960s – is the director solely responsible for a film's meaning? Some of these issues are addressed in this guide in relation to the case study directors, but the following provides a brief summary of the limitations of *auteur* theory that students should consider:

- The work of an *auteur* can be seen as an essentially collaborative process: eg To what extent is Wong Kar-Wai's reputation tied to the contributions made to his work by cinematographer Christopher Doyle and stylist William Chang? Similarly, students could consider the significance of the working partnership of Claire Denis with the director of photography Agnès Godard, which provides, as Denis puts it, 'a lot of security that allows you to explore'. (Darke 2000, p18).
- The cult status afforded to some *auteurs* and the exploitation of this by the film industry itself in terms of publicising and marketing their films. The case study of Lukas Moodysson (see pp55–58) indicates his increasing profile as a result of the cult following of his first two films. This led to a wider co-financing and distribution network for his third film, *Lilya 4-Ever* (2002). The pitfalls of wider financial participation and its impact on an *auteur*'s cult status are addressed in the case study of Lars von Trier (see pp58–64).
- Linked with this is the idea of the *auteur* as a trademark, to be used as a device to raise audience expectation for their next film, even if, as in the case of Wong Kar-Wai cited above, there is no predictable format or genre. What may be exploited in these instances is an elevation of the *auteur* as working outside the mainstream, specifically within the art-house circuit as discussed in the section on Art cinema (see pp20–4).
- The historic and cultural context of *auteur* films and their subsequent reappraisal. It is interesting to read retrospective accounts of the work of an *auteur* (eg Hitchcock) that offer a more reflective perspective on a career compared to contemporary views of a director's work.

● Stars

It is useful to revisit the idea of the star at A2 Level through the prism of World cinema.

The case study films highlight different approaches to stardom and what this contributes to an understanding of a national cinema: eg the Chinese actor Chow Yun-Fat has enjoyed crossover success in the international hit *Crouching Tiger Hidden Dragon* (Ang Lee, 2000, Hong Kong/China/Taiwan/USA). The *Time Out Film Guide*, in reviewing his first US role in *The Replacement Killers* (Antoine Fuqua, 1998, USA) describes Chow Yun-Fat as 'one of the world's coolest stars, *despite never having made an American movie* (my emphasis)'. (Pym, 2003, p1003) The review speaks of Chow Yun-Fat's 'iconic status' and the studio's need to capitalise on the success of his working partnership with John Woo in the Hong Kong films *The Killer* (1989) and *Hard-Boiled* (1992), which also featured Tony Leung, another well-known Hong Kong actor. Wong Kar-Wai has worked consistently with Tony Leung and a number of other Hong Kong actors, but tends not to present them in 'starring roles'.

By contrast, we might also consider the role of the Hollywood star in European films. The case study of Scandinavia highlights the international profile of Danish director Lars von Trier working with, among others, Nicole Kidman in his 2003 release *Dogville*. What added value does a star such as Kidman, who has worked in both the mainstream and independent US sectors, bring to a European film, albeit one made in the English language?

Conclusion

This chapter has addressed some of the key issues in the study of World cinema and can be adapted to consideration of other national cinemas.

- Bear in mind that the concepts highlighted are a basis for an exploration of World cinema. While evidence of understanding of these concepts is welcome in exams and coursework, examiners are looking for a critical personal engagement with the topics and independent thinking.
- There is potential here for Internet research by students, either in independent study or in group activities. Some websites are suggested at the end of this guide (Useful Websites, p88), but, as a starting point, http://imdb.com contains information about and links to films' and directors' websites. A good way to approach this, given the amount of information available, is to ask for specific background material: reviews of the film; nominations and awards at film festivals; biographical detail about the director; exhibition strategy and box-office performance, etc. Compare this to a Hollywood high-concept film that may have been released the same day, probably on a far higher number of screens and with much advance publicity.
- If you are in a situation where Internet access is restricted, you could compile your own study guide on a particular film or national cinema, from a range of materials available on the Internet and in film magazines. Ask students to consider questions using this material, including some 'what if' questions (eg 'What if this film had Hollywood backing?' 'How might it be marketed?' 'Whom could we cast in it?'). This is an enjoyable, creative strategy for fixing concepts in students' minds.

- You may find it better to focus on two or three concepts in detail, from which others would naturally emerge, eg exploiting the links between audience and spectatorship, or *auteur* and *mise en scène*.
- Examiners are looking for close analysis of appropriate film sequences, preferably chosen by the students themselves. The best candidates are able to imply a wider knowledge of the film's context when discussing its textual features. To achieve this you could narrow the focus: students could take the close study film and select one or two of the topics outlined in this chapter; this should lead them to a broader consideration of how these themes impact on the film's textual features.

3

Case studies: national cinemas

This section focuses on four national cinemas at varying stages of recognition and development.

- Hong Kong's reintegration into China in 1997 generated the cultural setting for a new phase in Chinese filmmaking. The work of Wong Kar-Wai in Hong Kong, particularly his films *Chungking Express* and *In the Mood for Love*, exemplifies how a cinematic New Wave can emerge in a country, under specific cultural and historical circumstances.
- The national cinemas of Sweden and Denmark have enjoyed a higher profile since the mid-1990s, due in part to the films of Swedish director Lukas Moodysson, whose *Show Me Love* is one of the case study films. Similarly, the work of the Dogme 95 group, originating in Denmark, has brought us some of the most notable cinema releases of the 1990s, including *The Idiots*.
- France provides us with an example of a more consistently high-profile European national cinema. Typical of the films in the 1990s, many of which tackled social issues, is *La Haine*. *Beau travail* offers a useful contrast, not least because of the background of its director.

Case Study 1: Hong Kong

In 1997, when the UK government returned its colony Hong Kong to China, there was considerable anxiety in the city-state about its future prosperity and stability. This situation can be explored through the films of the period, providing students with a strong basis for contextual study.

Hong Kong cinema is also important from the point of view of the variety of films made and, in some cases, their export value to the West. John Woo's success as a crossover director in both Hong Kong and the West means he has achieved the ultimate accolade of working in both the Far East and in Hollywood. Such scenarios raise questions of representation and how to place a director such as Woo.

Finally, Hong Kong cinema provides an example of a cinematic New Wave, emerging at a time when many critics thought that the new was no longer possible in cinema. This is largely due to the work of the director Wong Kar-Wai. This case study allows us to consider Wong Kar-Wai's place as an *auteur* within an emerging faction of Hong Kong cinema.

● Context and historical background

The 1970s and 1980s saw Hong Kong films gain genuine popularity in the West for the first time, with martial arts stars Bruce Lee and Jackie Chan becoming international cultural icons. At the same time, directors such as King Hu, Tsui Hark and John Woo attracted critical praise for their imaginative fusions of personal concerns and popular genres. By the 1990s, many Hong Kong filmmakers had also worked in Hollywood, and their action films in particular started to show a strong stylistic influence.

Contemporary Hong Kong cinema can be understood in a number of ways, especially through its cultural relationship with China, especially since their reunification in 1997. It remains to be seen which will be the dominant partner in Chinese cinema. Will China constitute a new audience for Hong Kong films, or will Hong Kong directors have to assimilate this new cultural and political relationship, and how will this affect their work?

In 2002, the Hong Kong and Chinese governments signed an agreement that gave Hong Kong films greater access to the mainland market, by exempting them from from mainland quota restrictions and no longer regarding them as 'foreign'. Instead, films co-produced by Hong Kong and the mainland would be classified as mainland films, opening up the market in terms of the range of subject matter that could be filmed and distribution rights, and providing greater employment opportunities for Hong Kong production staff.

N K Leung (1998) has described several trends in Hong Kong cinema leading up to the reunification, including:

- The coexistence of two languages within one cinema: films were made in both Cantonese (the Chinese dialect spoken in Hong Kong and Southern China) and in Mandarin (the dialect of Northern China);
- A cultural tension which generated diverse approaches to genre films, such as social realism, melodrama and musicals, in part due to the periodic emigration of filmmakers from China to Hong Kong during the 1930s and 1940s;
- The Cultural Revolution in China in 1966 with rioting in Hong Kong resulted in a stark demarcation between China and Hong Kong. Film production in the Cantonese language ceased and films were only made in Mandarin. As Leung puts it, 'it was as though the people of Hong Kong had lost their voice or the desire to speak in their own language' (1998, p554).

- The Mirror Phase of the late 1960s to early 1970s saw a self-reflexive cinema in which Hong Kong focused on its own image, seemingly oblivious to the future Chinese presence;
- The post-1997 consciousness period, a time when Hong Kong films implicitly addressed uncertainties over its future.

In more recent times, China has become a lucrative market for Hollywood studios. In December 2002, the Warner Bros studio announced that it was to finance its first Chinese language film, *Turn Left, Turn Right*, written and directed by the Hong Kong partnership of Johnnie To and Wai Ka-Fai. This was their first collaboration with a US studio. The film is to be made in Hong Kong and mainland China, and is viewed by Warner Bros as an opportunity to enter a lucrative film marketplace.

Warner Bros is the second US studio to enter Chinese-language film production, following the overwhelming success of Sony Pictures Entertainment's co-production of *Crouching Tiger, Hidden Dragon*. This film enjoyed both critical and box-office success, gaining a record 16 nominations at the Hong Kong Film Awards of 2001. The second most-nominated film (with 12 nominations), Wong Kar-Wai's *In the Mood for Love*, was quite different.

Interest from Hollywood has other implications, however, for the indigenous industry. As Stephen Teo said: 'the Hong Kong film industry is in crisis … its market share has shrunk by as much as 40% and box-office earnings have dropped. Ironically, as Hong Kong cinema has become better known internationally, its predominance in the domestic market has been eroded by Hollywood. In 1993, the year when the crisis can be said to have begun, *Jurassic Park* became the highest-grossing film of all time at the Hong Kong box office.' (1997, pvii)

● Characteristics of Hong Kong cinema

The most well-known and popular kind of Hong Kong cinema in the West is the action–martial arts genre exemplified by directors such as John Woo and actors such as Chow Yun-Fat (one of the stars of *Crouching Tiger, Hidden Dragon*). Their crossover success seems to lie in the hybrid nature of the films – the combination of East meets West, as described by Woo:

> … the design for the gun battles and action scenes in *A Better Tomorrow* [1986], which reinvented the gangster genre, combined elements from Hollywood Westerns and Chinese swordplay movies – the former revolving around opposites continually confronting one another, and the latter involving the use of martial arts choreography. (quoted in Odham Stokes and Hoover, 2001, p35)

Courtesy of *bfi* Stills

Chungking Express

In contrast to these films are those of the Hong Kong director Wong Kar-Wai, part of the Hong Kong New Wave, whose work has been compared with that of the French New Wave director Jean-Luc Godard. Unlike the more commercial Hong Kong films, Wong Kar-Wai's films are not easy to place. *In the Mood for Love* has all the characteristics of Art cinema (see pp20–4), a style which has yet to be fully accepted in Hong Kong. It also has much in common with more commercial Hong Kong films, in that it features actors who have appeared in both Far East and Hollywood films. For example, Tony Leung, who starred in Wong Kar-Wai's *Happy Together* (1997, Hong Kong) is also to be found in John Woo's *Hard-Boiled* see **Worksheet 6**.

In line with the more 'elite' aspects of Hong Kong cinema is Wong Kar-Wai's *Chungking Express*, a film that enjoyed 'cult' status on its release in the UK in 1994 due to its unconventional filmic style and narrative pattern. *Chungking Express* is an example of a film that gained its reputation through word of mouth rather than a high-profile publicity campaign. The comparisons with Godard here arise through the film's alternative narrative style and fresh use of editing and cinematography. It took just three months to make and this is reflected in its seemingly spontaneous style. The film was successful in Asia and has found an audience in the West, through the art-house circuit and its release on DVD.

Despite the exuberance of the film, it discloses the underside of Hong Kong and is a kind of micro-study of the life of a city. **Worksheet 7** enables students to investigate this. It includes the results of a 1997 survey of critics with a specialist interest in Hong Kong cinema, as well as a quotation by one critic that will enable students to address some critical responses to *Chungking Express*.

The activities in **Worksheet 7** can be adapted for investigating other films in your specification. Take a quote as a starting point – preferably one your students might take issue with – and see what the response is. Questions can be phrased that will meet the criteria of your particular exam specification. For example, A2 Film Studies requires, as a starting point, consideration of messages and values that arise from the film text and how this is achieved cinematically.

1 of 2 pages

Worksheet 8 offers suggestions on how students can undertake Internet research on Wong Kar-Wai, and connect the look and style of his films with their distribution and exhibition history. In doing this they will make the text/context connection required by the Film Studies specification.

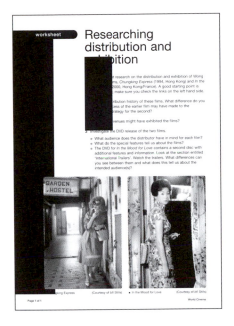

● Wong Kar-Wai as an auteur

John Woo has enjoyed critical and commercial success by combining aspects of East and West to reinvent popular genre films. By contrast, Wong Kar-Wai has enjoyed international acclaim despite his films being difficult to place in terms of style. Trick cinematography and editing are used in an experimental way, contributing to the 'cool factor'. What the films lack, however, are clear narrative signposts in terms of characterisation, cause and effect, and their endings are open to a number of interpretations.

In introducing *Chungking Express* to your students, you could point to Quentin Tarantino's endorsement of it on the DVD cover; for some students, this would represent the ultimate accolade. You could also ask them to consider how it references American culture through Western images. In this way it could be compared to *À Bout de souffle*. McDonald's and Coca-Cola feature as part of the Hong Kong consumer landscape. American pop music such as the Mamas and the Papas 'California Dreaming' provides the cultural backdrop to the film, and Faye's desire to leave Hong Kong for the supposedly better life offered by California, keeps her in her dead-end job at the café which Cop 663 ultimately takes over.

In the Mood for Love, by contrast, attracted much quieter critical acclaim on its release in 2000, winning Best Actor and Technical Awards at Cannes that year, though it went on to gain 24 awards and a further 19 nominations. This is a film aimed fairly and squarely at the Art cinema market in Europe in its form and style, and its marketing, distribution and exhibition reflect this. Students could also consider the film's release on DVD in June 2001, the marketing campaign for which was stronger than for its cinema distribution. Advertisements were placed in *Sight and Sound* for the Director's Special Edition, consisting of a two-disc DVD boxed set with attendant extras, and its distribution by Metro Tartan Video again signposts the film as belonging in the World cinema section of the high-street retailer. What does this suggest about its intended audience (see pp28–9)?

Wong Kar-Wai's films have enjoyed varying degrees of success in Hong Kong itself. *Chungking Express* was a surprise hit, despite the Hong Kong audience's preference for genre films and the director's casting of well-known indigenous stars in unusual roles.

Central to the requirements of A Level Film Studies is the need for close textual analysis of relevant film sequences, demonstrating understanding of the issues raised. An example is contained on **Worksheet 9**, which can be used as the basis of textual analysis of the opening sequence from *In the Mood for Love* and/or *Chungking Express*. Students should consider the opening sequence in the context of the early 1990s, when the film was made. How does it reflect the film's central themes of separation, uncertainty and reunification?

The sensual slow-motion shots which open *Chungking Express*, showing a cop in plain clothes chasing a drug suspect in Hong Kong's lively hub of Asian multiculturalism … signal a slow recognition that the Hong Kong new wave is coming full circle. *Chungking Express* is an expression of the convergence of Hong Kong's post-modern aesthetics and a curiously old-fashioned, but not outmoded, romanticism. Wong's work to date sums up the circuitous development of the Hong Kong new wave. However, the film doesn't look back as much as it attempts to push forward. Indeed, at times Wong even seems to be shoving a new genre at his audience: a post-modern romance, a new wave editing style, on-location realism and narrative dissonance. (Teo, 2001, p196).

This approach can be adapted to your own choice of film. The important thing is to anchor the internal features of the film with:

- The context in which it was made (cultural, political, historical); and
- The messages and values (or representational issues) offered by the film.

● Summary

To summarise, the following issues should be considered in a study of Hong Kong cinema:

- The contextual and historical place of national cinema in the light of Hong Kong's recent reunification with China;
- The general perception of Hong Kong cinema as characterised by genre-based, action films;
- The success of the films at home and abroad;
- The environment and context in which an *auteur*, such as Wong Kar-Wai, can function;
- The subsequent career of your chosen *auteur* within his or her national cinema and beyond;
- The international audience for Hong Kong cinema.

You can apply these issues in broad terms to other examples of national cinema in a consideration of World cinema.

Case Study 2: Sweden and Denmark

Taking Scandinavian cinema as a case study allows us to investigate aspects of a national cinema currently enjoying a renaissance. With this in mind, how do we place the two Scandinavian countries featured here, Sweden and Denmark, within the categories European cinema and World cinema?

The national and European success of the films featured here has led to a widening of their market into other territories, which will lead us to consider issues to do with production, distribution and exhibition.

● Context and historical background

While greater recognition has been given to the development of early cinema in Britain, France and the USA, the Scandinavian countries were also instrumental in the development of film from around 1910, both as an art form and, crucially, as an industry, with its artistic and commercial links with Germany.

The establishment of the film studio Nordisk Film Kompagni in 1907, the second-largest in the world after Pathé, enabled Denmark to become a major player on the world stage. It produced ground-breaking new genres, what Paolo Cherchi Usai has termed the '"sensationalist" film, set in the world of crime, vice or the circus' (Cherchi Usai, 1997, p154). As a consequence of this, new developments in lighting, cinematography, set design and special effects for creating the right look for crime films.

Courtesy of *bfi* Stills

Show me Love

Denmark also influenced on other film-producing countries from around 1910 onwards. Early films by directors such as Mauritz Stiller and Victor Sjöström made prior to 1916 'bear the technical imprint of Denmark' (Cherchi Usai, 1997, p155). Most notable were techniques that came to be associated with Expressionistic lighting, combined with expertise in set design such as the framing of characters to create silhouettes, both of which became features of Russian cinema during this period. The influence of Denmark can also be closely linked with German cinema during the 1910s and 1920s. Cherchi Usai connects the 'sensational' themes of Danish cinema with an Expressionist aesthetic that can subsequently be seen in the early films of Fritz Lang.

The Danish film industry fell into decline after World War I, although the country's most notable filmmaker, Carl Theodor Dreyer, continued to work in other European countries where he made, for example, *The Passion of Joan of Arc* (1928, France) and *Vampyr* (1932, Germany/France).

The formation of studios with both an artistic and commercial framework meant that Sweden similarly enjoyed success in the early years of cinema. In particular, Svensk Filmindustri had become an international success by 1920 and was largely instrumental in a golden age of Swedish cinema from 1916 to 1921. This success was due, according to Cherchi Usai, in part to Sweden's neutrality during the Great War and its subsequent freedom in distributing its films worldwide and in part to capitalising on a reduced import market. Sweden was to become, to some extent, a victim of its own success by the departure of its most notable stars and directors for Hollywood (Greta Garbo and Victor Sjöström among them), as well as the increasing demand for Hollywood films in Sweden itself.

Hollywood films continue to be popular in Scandinavia, although the national cinemas are now enjoying a renaissance, not least through the formation of mini-studios which recall the structure of the early years of Swedish cinema. The town of Trollhättan has been dubbed 'Trollywood' because of the number of films made there recently. Lukas Moodysson, however, who made *Show Me Love*, *Together* and *Lilya 4-Ever* there, has strongly rejected this nickname, as he sees the industry there as the complete antithesis of Hollywood and everything it stands for (Tom de Castella, *Sight and Sound*, vol 14, no 1, p8). Despite the crassness of the nickname, it is nevertheless recognition of the vibrancy and productive nature of the current Swedish film industry.

This resource includes suggestions for extending a close study topic, eg in Film Studies, to a more general research area in Media Studies. For example, the Swedish film *Show Me Love* is a close study film on the WJEC A2 Film Studies specification (from June 2004) that can be broadened in the following way:

- Director Lukas Moodysson as *auteur*;
- Moodysson as a director working within the Swedish film industry;
- Swedish cinema as part of Scandinavian cinema;
- Scandinavian cinema as European cinema;
- Scandinavian cinema's role in Europe's impact on the rest of the world;
- Scandinavia as part of World cinema.

Case study 2a: Sweden

Sweden has enjoyed a resurgence of interest and success in its domestic market since the late 1990s, gaining a higher profile through success in international film festivals (including nominations for an Oscar™). This has been largely due to the success of the filmmaker Lukas Moodysson, whose films *Show Me Love*, *Together* and *Lilya 4-Ever* have been successful beyond Sweden itself.

In 2000, a record number of 35 films were made, nine by first-time directors. Although this may still seem quite a small number, bear in mind the Swedish population is only 8.5 million. By contrast Britain, (population 59 million) which has a much more established film profile as well as a larger export 'industry', made only 98 films in the same year, more than 40 of which received some funding from the relatively new Lottery fund.

We can now put this in the context of the first case study example in this section. Lukas Moodysson's first film, *Show Me Love*, was produced in Sweden, while his latest film, *Lilya 4-Ever*, was a co-production between Sweden and Denmark. What's more, Moodysson's second film, *Together*, was a co-production between Sweden, Denmark and Italy. Considering this gives an indication of the problems relating to defining a film purely in terms of its country of origin.

● Some background to Swedish cinema

The resurgence of a new Swedish cinema in 2000 can be explained, in part at least, by changes in legislation, which allowed the industry to receive more benefits, enabling new directors to exhibit films. The legislation gave more recognition to films either made by immigrant directors or to films which address issues centring on immigration. Some of these have reached a wider audience, winning awards at the San Sebastian film festival, as well as the European Council's Iris Prize for Best Multi-Cultural Programme. This is significant bearing in mind that of a population of 8.5 million, 1.5 million are from ethnic minorities. This resurgence has impacted on the market for indigenous films. In 2000, domestic productions were 25 per cent of the domestic market. During the first two months of 2001, 46 per cent of the population chose to see a Swedish film.

The Swedish Film Institute reported that in 2002, cinema attendance in Sweden increased for the fifth year running. The total attendance amounted to 18.3 million. Revenues in 2002 increased by four per cent, the seventh consecutive year of increase. Part of this is due to the import market of films such as *The Lord of the Rings: The Fellowship of the Ring* (Peter Jackson, 2001, USA/New Zealand), but Swedish films are holding out against the competition. *Lilya 4-Ever* was the fourth most successful Swedish film in Sweden in 2002 and won five major awards in Sweden's equivalent of the Oscars in 2003. For up-to-date information on the Swedish film industry, it is worth referring to the Swedish Film Institute website, www.sfi.se.

● Lukas Moodysson as an *auteur*

Moodysson has been championed as the director to spearhead a renaissance in Swedish cinema. The revival of Swedish cinema followed the success of *Show Me Love* in 1998, and is referred to in *Sight and Sound* magazine as the 'Moodysson effect' (Macnab, 2001, p33). However, Moodyson's outspoken nature has not endeared him to the Swedish film establishment, despite the critical and popular success of his films.

As befits the work of an *auteur*, Moodysson's films are highly personal projects. *Together*, in particular, was informed by the political climate prevalent in Sweden during his childhood. Counter to the (now) traditional style of New Wave films characterised by the use of handheld cameras, Moodysson's signature style is the use of mainly fixed camera positions with zooms for added effect.

● *Show Me Love*

The following information and suggestions may help in the study of *Show Me Love*, providing a basis for textual analysis and reinforcing the link between a film as a text and its context of production (pp33–38). See **Worksheet 10**.

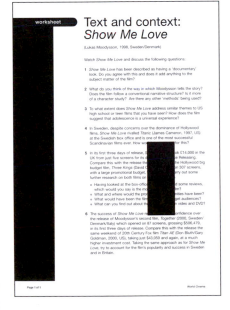

- *Show Me Love* has the characteristics of documentary or video diary style, focusing on teenage angst and preoccupations. The style is enhanced by the use of natural lighting and grainy footage, as if the girls were filming themselves with their own video cameras.
- Students may like to consider the contribution the look and style adds to the message of the film. Would the film's impact be the same if it were filmed in a more conventional way?
- The use of everyday locations lends the film a low-budget look and feel.
- Moodysson is taking an exploratory approach here, concentrating on character development, rather than narrative as such.
- The subject matter is familiar from Hollywood teen/high school films, but *Show Me Love* takes a different approach. The film captures the boredom of teenage existence, a sense of time passing slowly, with the feeling that everything is happening elsewhere. (The film's Swedish title is *Fucking Åmål*, a reference to the tedium of living in the town, Åmål, in which it is set.)

- Despite concerns over the dominance of Hollywood films, *Show Me Love* rivalled *Titanic* (James Cameron, 1997, USA) at the Swedish box office and is one of the most successful Scandinavian films ever.

- The film raises questions about the distribution of foreign-language films in the UK and their success relative to their promotion and exhibition. *Show Me Love* took £14,000 in the UK from just five screens for distributor Alliance Releasing in its first three days of release. Compare this with the release the same week of the big-budget Hollywood film *Three Kings* (David O Russell, 1999, US) on 307 screens, with a large promotional budget, taking just £1.4m. (Students could also consider why its original title might work in Sweden, but wouldn't be acceptable to distributors in the UK.)

- As a film by a then unknown director, *Show Me Love* opened in Sweden with 35 prints, taking $483,626 during its first week and grossing $6,457,137 in total. It is one of the top ten highest-grossing films in Norway with a total gross of $3m.

- As a result of the success of *Show Me Love*, there was more confidence over the release of Moodysson's second film, *Together*, which opened on 87 screens grossing $506,479 in its first three days of release. Compare this with the release the same weekend of the Twentieth-Century Fox film *Titan AE* (Don Bluth, Gary Goldman, 2000), which flopped, taking just $43,059 against a much higher investment cost. (Buddrus, 2000)

- **Textual analysis of *Show Me Love***

The following suggestions for a textual analysis on *Show Me Love* focus on messages and values, or representation: who and what is being shown, and how effective are the cinematic devices? They include consideration of the synoptic units required for A2 Film Studies which will also have relevance for other exam specifications requiring a textual, contextual or representational approach. **Worksheet 11** offers students the opportunity to consider these scenes with synoptic units in mind.

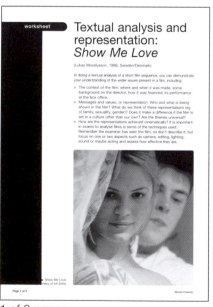

1 of 2 pages

The main themes here are universal: images of bored teenagers, time standing still, unrequited love and parents who don't understand – all typify the teenage high school genre exemplified by US films from *Rebel without a Cause* (Nicholas Ray, 1955, USA) to *Cruel Intentions* (Roger Kumble, 1999, USA).

- In class, discuss the genre conventions of such films, considering of *mise en scène*, camerawork, sound and narrative structure.
- The second scene raises issues concerning messages and values in the film. The family is represented on Elin's sixteenth birthday, through that most intimate and yet intrusive of devices, the home video camera, filming in apparently natural light and in a seemingly amateur fashion. **Worksheet 11** allows students to consider how the low-budget look of this scene supports both its style and its message.
- The scene which follows shows Agnes as the object of male attention – a neat contrast with the sense we get of Elin's solitude, despite being surrounded by her family.
- We then see Agnes in discussion with her father; he is eager to please, she is trying to say the right things, both realising what the other is doing. The style here is more formal and conventional. Students should pick up on the shot-reverse-shot technique in mid-shot here to record a conversation, intercut with zooms onto particular objects, eg the party invitation, which looms large as an object of contention.
- A later scene in the film (35 minutes in) is a pivotal one as it subverts the power relationships set up at the beginning of the film. Agnes returns to Elin's house to apologise for humiliating her. They then leave the house, heading for another party. It is at this point that Elin's status as the object of suspicion and derision is starting to change with the growing admiration she receives from Agnes. While Agnes had previously been shown as desirable and confident, the centre of attention, Elin, by contrast, seemed introverted and marginalised, the new girl who found it hard to integrate with the rest of the class, the unpopular teenager familiar from US high school films. When the two girls reconcile, this power relationship is subtly overturned to reveal Elin as more confident of her sexual identity as Agnes becomes more in awe of her.
- As the two leave Elin's home, the true desolation of the town of Åmål is revealed. Shot at night with hand-held cameras, the girls are seen crossing the bridge from Åmål to the motorway, where they hope to hitch a lift to Stockholm, representing perhaps the divide between what they are leaving behind and a more exciting future, implicit in city life.
- Expectations in relation to genre recognition are being confirmed and yet subverted here; we have the convention of the young, blonde object of desire by two characters, only one of whom is male, the other the ugly duckling female who nevertheless gets her (in this case) woman.

Show Me Love lacks the more conspicuous style of a film such as *Chungking Express*, but nevertheless textual analysis will address the ways in which the text supports issues of representation in the film.

- Do students feel that this is a different kind of cinema from the ones with which they are familiar? Is the theme of the film a universal story? Could the film have been made in the UK and, if so, by whom and starring whom?
- Do students perceive this and other Moodysson films as being part of a New Wave or is this term becoming overused? Moodysson is arguably the first major director of international note to emerge from Sweden since Ingmar Bergman and is largely responsible for the recent upturn in the Swedish film industry's fortunes. Does his style seem fresh, the low-budget look which typifies the French New Wave, for example? Or is the use of hand-held camera and the documentary look something we have all seen before which is now becoming part of the mainstream, especially given its ubiquitous use on television? Is there anything else distinctive or ground-breaking about the style or content of the film?
- What issues of sexuality are present within *Show Me Love* and how are they dealt with?

Case study 2b: Denmark

Danish cinema is also a film industry enjoying a revival at home and abroad. Government money for films, monitored by the Danish Film Institute, increased from DKK200 million per year in 1998 to DKK350 million in 2001. Expenditure includes projects such as the promotion of Danish films abroad (eg Sheffield has hosted a Danish film festival).

In 1999 a record number of cinemagoers in Denmark chose to see Danish films, with national productions making up 28 per cent of the box office. A number of awards at international film festivals helped to make 2000 an even better year. Director Lars von Trier won the Palme d'Or at Cannes for *Dancer in the Dark*, as well as the European Film Academy Award for Best Film. Von Trier's wide media coverage in Denmark and beyond resulted in considerable exposure for Danish cinema.

In 2000, *Italian for Beginners* (Denmark/Sweden), directed by Lone Scherfig, was released in Denmark to critical acclaim and seen by 10 per cent of the population in its first six weeks. Made by Lars von Trier's production company, Zentropa, *Italian for Beginners* cost just Euro 1.9 million, but won awards at the Berlin Festival in 2001, received wide distribution across Europe and enjoyed a record-breaking number of box-office admissions.

A key factor in the recent international success of Danish cinema is Dogme 95, some would argue the most influential movement in World cinema for a generation. Dogme 95 was started by four Danish directors who wrote a radical manifesto to take filmmaking back to basics, including the following criteria: stories must be set in the present and films must be shot on location, with a handheld camera, using natural light and direct sound (see pXX for full manifesto).

Dogme 95 was launched internationally in 1998 at the Cannes Film Festival, when Martin Scorsese's jury awarded a top prize to Thomas Vinterberg's *Festen* (Denmark/Sweden), a disturbing story of sexual abuse in an upper-class family. The success of the Dogme 95 films has resulted in a shift from home territory, as reflected in the 2003 release of Thomas Vinterberg's new film *It's All about Love*, funded by contributions from eight different countries. The film provides a useful case study in considering the nationality of a foreign language film and the impact on a national cinema, when an indigenous film and its director enjoy international success.

Courtesy of *bfi* Stills

Festen

- *It's All about Love* was made with support from Danish, English, French, Swedish, Japanese, Italian, German and Greek financing.
- It cost Euro 11.5 million to make.
- It was pre-sold to some 90 countries.
- It was made in the English language.
- It stars Claire Danes and Joaquin Phoenix, two rising Hollywood stars.
- The Danish Film Institute website (www.dfi.dk) claims the film as Danish because its director, Thomas Vinterberg, produced it through his production company, Nimbus Film.

The Danish Film Institute website provides further resource material which will help you to plan and develop your own activities with students. They could, for example, trace the production history of the latest film by the Dogme95 directors, particularly as they continue to become more of an international brand. A research project on Lars von Trier would also be interesting, and students could consider the extent to which his signature can be identified when working within the terms of the Dogme 95 manifesto.

The Idiots has a number of applications across the WJEC A2 Film Studies specification and can form the basis for developing other World cinema topics, for example:

- Director Lars von Trier as an *auteur*;
- Denmark, along with Sweden, as part of a cinematic New Wave;
- *The Idiots* as Art cinema (pp20–24), raising issues of distribution etc;
- Danish cinema as a film industry enjoying a revival in Denmark and beyond.

● How to use *The Idiots*

Including *The Idiots* in a Film or Media Studies programme provides a good opportunity for teachers and students to subvert and reconsider many issues already covered. Cinematic methods, such as editing, use of the camera, sound or *mise en scène*, can be compared and contrasted with the kinds of anti-techniques associated with the Dogme 95 group.

The Idiots

Be warned, however, that *The Idiots* contains graphic sexual scenes which you may consider inappropriate for students at AS Level, and a full screening of the film would not in any case suit the requirements of this early stage of study. Less controversial scenes from the film could be selected to demonstrate the flip side of continuity editing, unobtrusive camerawork, post-production sound and artificial lighting.

Dogme 95 was set up by four Danish filmmakers: Lars von Trier, Thomas Vinterberg, Søren Kragh-Jacobsen and Kristian Levring. The intention was to challenge and subvert the whole premise on which films were made – a back-to-basics approach. Informing this is the Dogme 95 manifesto itself, a list of ten 'rules' which must be adhered to in order to establish a common identity across the films. The rules are really a list of anti-rules.

You could show a clip from *The Idiots* (perhaps the 'house purchase' and 'Christmas decoration' sequences about one hour into the film) and ask students to identify what the ten rules might be, taking the approach that they are 'anti-rules'. **Worksheet 12** lists the ten rules:

The ten rules of Dogme 95:
I swear to submit to the following set of rules drawn up and confirmed by Dogme 95.

1. Shooting must be done on location. Props and sets must not be brought in (if a particular prop is necessary for the story, a location must be chosen where this prop is to be found).
2. The sound must never be produced apart from the images or vice versa. (Music must not be used unless it occurs where the scene is being shot.)
3. The camera must be handheld. Any movement or immobility attainable in the hand is permitted. (The film must not take place where the camera is standing; shooting must take place where the film takes place.)
4. The film must be in colour. Special lighting is not acceptable. (If there is too little light for exposure the scene must be cut or a single lamp be attached to the camera.)
5. Optical work and filters are forbidden.
6. The film must not contain superficial action. (Murders, weapons, etc must not occur.)
7. Temporal and geographical alienation are forbidden. (That is to say that the film takes place here and now.)
8. Genre movies are not acceptable.
9. The film format must be Academy 35 mm.
10. The director must not be credited.

Copenhagen, Monday 13 March 1995
On behalf of Dogme 95
(Roberts and Wallis, 2001, p98)

Worksheet 12 also provides some contextual background to the film and asks students to consider the criteria offered by Susan Hayward for what defines Art cinema (pp20–24). It would seem that *The Idiots* and other films of the Dogme 95 school fit into this category; but is it quite that simple? Added to this is Hayward's view of Art cinema as the natural developing ground for *auteurs*; again, von Trier's approach would fit into the definition offered in Section 2 (pp38–41). The challenge for students is whether they can identify von Trier as being different from mainstream directors (in my experience, they do) and recognise

an *auteurist* vision as explained in Section 2. Von Trier is noteworthy in this respect in that he also directed the more mainstream English-language film *Breaking the Waves* (1996, Denmark/Sweden/France/Netherlands/Norway) starring the British actress Emily Watson.

Worksheet 13 invites students to investigate the success of a small company based in Denmark such as Nimbus Film (set up by Thomas Vinterberg) or Zentropa (set up by Lars von Trier) and asks them to devise their own film production company. What follows is some background to the success of these companies, which students can compare with their own.

● Nimbus Film
The three key personnel of Nimbus Film are Birgitte Hald and Bo Ehrhardt, both graduates of the National Film School of Denmark, and the director Thomas Vinterberg. They seem to have a winning combination: the creative triangle of director, scriptwriter and producer attaining great success with their choice of talent and scripts.

Nimbus Film's success can be attributed to a willingness to support young talented filmmakers (which, on a practical level, would be relatively inexpensive) and include the first film made under the Dogme 95 manifesto, *Festen* made by Vinterberg in 1998. It won the Jury Prize at Cannes that year. The following year, *Mifune* (Søren Kragh-Jacobsen) won the Silver Bear in Berlin. Both of these films had outstanding reviews in Denmark and beyond.

● Zentropa
  Lars von Trier and Peter Aalbeck Jensen, both graduates of the National Film School of Denmark, established Zentropa in 1992. The Danish Film Institute website references *Screen* magazine's appraisal of the company as

  > the creative and business powerhouse that has invigorated an industry with its Dogme 95 concept, produced seminal works such as von Trier's *Breaking the Waves* and *Dancer in the Dark* and turned the Zentropa name into a brand itself, with international buyers, producers and directors eagerly awaiting its next move. Zentropa continues to be a prolific, versatile and visionary player within the film sector. (www.dfi.dk).

● Like Nimbus Film, Zentropa has encouraged new directors with original ideas and scripts, as well as supporting more established names within Danish cinema.

● *Breaking the Waves* was the first of three films by von Trier to be acclaimed at the Cannes Film Festival. Its success was followed by the awarding of the Palme d'Or to *Dancer in the Dark*.

● Lars von Trier's film *Dogville* (2003), at a cost of Euro 11.2 million, is an international co-production starring Nicole Kidman, Lauren Bacall, James Caan, Ben Gazzara and Stellan Skarsgård, about as unusual and varied a cast as a director could hope to accumulate. How can we now place von Trier as a director of World cinema?

The Idiots can also be used to explore the following:

● **Shocking cinema**: What is the shock element in *The Idiots*? Rather than the portrayal of sexuality, the subversive portrayal of disability in the film, which raises questions relating to messages and values, may challenge students more. **Worksheet 14** invites students to address some of these issues.

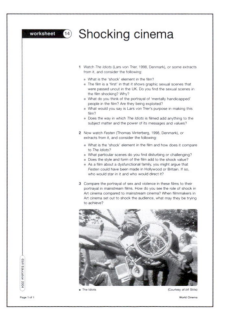

● **Regulation and censorship**: *The Idiots* is a landmark film in the history of British film classification and censorship. The British Board of Film Classification allowed scenes of male erection and genital penetration to be passed uncut on its cinema release and on video. A screening of the film on television is subject to ITC regulations, and when first shown on FilmFour, the channel decided to pixelate rather than delete graphic scenes, but compromised by allowing uncut scenes to be available on the FilmFour website. Eventually, however, on 14 July 2000, *The Idiots* was shown uncut and unpixelated, with no intervention from the ITC – a landmark in British broadcasting.

– What may cause more offence (possibly to parents rather than students) is the portrayal of disability, by what some would consider a group of middle-class dropouts.

– The film provides a case study of a key moment in British film classification history in allowing such scenes to be shown. The BBFC seemed more concerned that offence could be caused to disabled people and their families, but, in the end, ruled that the performances were acceptable within the context of the film.

– The *Banned* section of the FilmFour website (www.filmfour.com/banned) is an invaluable resource for specific films that have been subject to controversial decisions in the past. It also provides commentary by Mark Kermode, a fervent opponent of film censorship. It is the kind of website students love, containing reference to cult films such as *Trainspotting* and *Bad Lieutenant* (Abel Ferrara, 1992, USA), and providing concise background material.

– New guidelines were issued in 2000 by the BBFC concerning the portrayal of sex on screen, which is now permitted providing the scenes are brief and justified in the context. In a spirit of more apparent openness to public opinion, market research was undertaken on the suitability of such films on video with implications for home viewing.

– Several of the breakthrough films for the BBFC have been foreign-language films emerging from the art-house circuit, reflecting perhaps the less censorial context in which the films were made, certainly as far as the European films are concerned.

– The BBFC has its own website (www.bbfc.co.uk) which includes its policy on film classification, as well as a search facility for specific films.

● **Summary**

Sweden and Denmark can be understood as small national cinemas currently on the World cinema map. As they are enjoying a renaissance, they offer the opportunity for considering a number of issues relating to the areas of study in the exam specifications, such as:

- A reappraisal of national cinema including questions about the identity of a national cinema. Increasingly, Scandinavian films are becoming international co-productions, not least with Hollywood studios;
- Questions of authorship – eg How can we approach authorship in terms of the Scandinavian directors under investigation, both working within the Dogme 95 framework?
- Issues relating to art cinema – eg How does it support the work of *auteurs*? How does it extend the boundaries of what is shown in film and what challenges does this pose to censorship bodies?
- Questions of audience appeal – eg What kind of challenge do the films of Lars von Trier and Thomas Vinterberg present for international audiences?
- Questions of funding and distribution – eg Will future Dogme 95 films be financially successful relative to their investment, particularly with pressure from co-producers?

The above questions can be adapted for studying other European cinemas and their place on the world stage.

Case study 3: France

● Context and historical background

France is one of the major pioneers in the development of cinema, at both an industrial and artistic level. The early formation of production companies such as Pathé and Gaumont, combined with experimentation by, among others, the Lumière brothers and Georges Meliès, made France a key player in World cinema from its beginnings in the 1890s.

Courtesy of *bfi* Stills

Beau travail

The decline in popularity of French cinema during World War I was followed by a rise in experimental, avant-garde films, including the work of surrealist filmmakers such as René Clair. The 1930s have been acclaimed for the depiction of 'poetic realism', defined as 'a pessimistic, film noir type of populist drama blending surface realism (contemporary urban settings, working class characters) with poetic stylisation' (Kuhn, 1990, p164). This style was given a harder edge in the *policier* genre of the 1950s, typified by the films of Jean-Pierre Melville. This period also saw the formation of the group of writers-turned-directors who created French New Wave cinema.

Cinematic New Waves are considered as a general topic in Section 2 (pp26–28), and the case studies on Hong Kong, Denmark and Sweden consider featured directors as instrumental in the resurgence of their respective cinemas at specific times. The case studies highlight the importance of the contextual background of close study films, and French New Wave cinema of the late 1950s and 1960s provides a good example of films which emerged as a result of certain historical, technological and economic factors.

In *The Cinema Book* (2000), Pam Cook and Mieke Bernink trace the evolution of the French New Wave by reference to critical theory around its inception and development. Discussion centres on the contribution made by, among others, François Truffaut, whose own style of filmmaking emerged in response to a more traditional strand of French cinema of the 1940s. Truffaut sought to challenge this cinema through his writing and in the style of direction.

Essential elements of French New Wave films included techniques that challenged traditional notions and restricted artistic practices in filmmaking. New Wave filmmakers used long takes that captured the essence of a scene, rather than providing any narrative function; freeze frames to enhance character; jump cuts to subvert ideas relating to continuity in time and space. These new techniques provided, as Cook and Bernink suggest, 'a specific aesthetic system, a language in itself'. (2000, p81)

Terry Lovell offers an alternative to the aesthetic approach to French New Wave films, highlights the importance of economic, ideological and political factors. With a focus on the individual, Lovell notes that 'heroes are neither personally nor socially integrated, and are disassociated from their social roles. These are, in any case, difficult or impossible to identify.' Comparison can be made here with the case study films: Hong Kong cinema and Swedish and Danish cinema contain characters whose primary function seems to be to portray the isolated or marginal. These can be viewed alongside the representation of particular cultures in the films.

Lovell considers the social conditions from which French New Wave films emerged, citing:

the huge influx of American films upon the market immediately after the war, in the circumstances in which the American allies were also the liberators. This influx may have something to do with the near-obsession with all things American and especially with American movies, which the New Wave evidenced so strongly in both its films and in its critical judgments. (quoted in Cook and Bernink, 2000, p81)

Cook and Bernink however suggest that French films of this period engaged in direct competition with what could also be seen as a 'threat' to French culture. These films were also made with the aim of infiltrating the American and wider European markets. There are clear references to US culture in *À Bout de souffle* for example, while also offering the loose, fragmentary style is associated with Art cinema (see pp20–24).

● Approaching French cinema 1: *La Haine*

One way to start a study of French cinema is to gauge the understanding students have of the way in which cinema represents national identity (see pp8–9 and 25–26). French cinema offers opportunities to explore a film culture that students may perceive as being very different from British cinema.

Courtesy of *bfi* Stills

La Haine

Films set in France (often made by Hollywood studios) that have enjoyed success in the UK are virtually advertisements for French culture and landscapes. For example, images of Paris are often centred on the main tourist attractions – the use of the Eiffel Tower and Arc de Triomphe in *French Kiss* (Lawrence Kasdan, 1995, USA/UK) or *Forget Paris* (Billy Crystal, 1995, USA) – and depictions of peasant or rural life in films such as *Jean de Florette* and *Manon des Sources* (Claude Berri, 1986, France/Switzerland/Italy).

In contrast, some recent films have subverted this image. *La Haine*, directed by Mathieu Kassovitz and winner of the 1995 Best Director award at the Cannes Film Festival, presents a gritty urban setting and tone which does not serve as a promotional campaign for Paris. Indeed, its treatment of contemporary issues could be set in any city experiencing urban deprivation. On its release in 1995, *La Haine* was compared in *Sight and Sound* magazine to Spike Lee's 1989 film *Do the Right Thing*, because of its edgy, urban feel and setting which echoed *Do the Right Thing*'s Brooklyn district of New York. Lee's film addresses head on issues of race and racial segregation during one hot summer night. *La Haine* was popular in France and was distributed throughout Europe, including the UK, albeit primarily on the Art-house circuit. It received much critical acclaim, for its alternative take on French life and culture.

Students may recognise that *Do the Right Thing* has a distinctly American feel to it, in the style of urban youth clothing, its exploration of Black American popular hip-hop culture and the use of low-angle oblique shots to make it seem contemporary and real. With this in mind, is *La Haine* derivative of such films, or is it an original French film in its own right? **Worksheet 15** suggests a class activity to address this.

If possible, obtain a DVD copy of *La Haine* and show an extract without subtitles and with the sound turned down. Ask students how they would place the film in terms of time, location and context. For example, does it have the look of a film from America, Britain or a European country? How is France represented in the sequence? Does the use of camera and editing give the film a more American feel? (Exam questions often require students to link *what* is represented with the *way* it is represented in the film.)

Like *À Bout de souffle*, *La Haine* is firmly set within French society, yet references American culture, including music and film. Jill Forbes refers to it as a 'Zeitgeist film which sums up the mood and preoccupations of a particular time and place, but in a way that is internationally appealing' (2000, p171).

You could also consider issues of realism. Realism involves the conscious construction of a style, by technical and ideological processes, which connotes a sense of an unmediated or directly reflected reality, when really it is as constructed and contrived as any work of fiction or drama.

- To what extent do the form and style of the film give a 'reality effect'? Does the fact that it is shot in black and white, arguably giving it a documentary look, enhance or detract from this?
- To what extent does the use of black and white reinforce the film's subject matter? Would the film have the same impact had it been shot in colour?
- Consider the interlacing of fact and fiction. While the film is fictional, we seem to be intruding on the personal life of the three main characters, seeing the social issues from the protagonists' point of view. The film is based on real contemporary events – the housing estate is a symbol of economic decline, with high unemployment, especially among the young; drug dealing; gang warfare; and violent hatred of the police. Links can be made between representation and the cinematic devices used to achieve this.

Worksheet 15 provides suggestions for textual analysis on a scene of your students' choice. To what extent do they feel that the subject matter of *La Haine* is inextricably linked with its form and style. Would the overall effect be as powerful if it were filmed in a more conventional way? If you are also covering Danish cinema, you could compare the relationship between representation and form and style in this film and *The Idiots*.

As a starting point, you may wish to view the opening sequence:

- This is very powerful and looks almost surreal.
- The inclusion of actual news footage is effective in making fiction seem like fact.
- The director, Mathieu Kassovitz, has described the film as being 'anti-police': what evidence is there of this?
- Kassovitz presents messages and values in various ways, eg in the news report headline 'Riots allegedly because of police brutality. One protestor critically ill.' Issues of race, poverty etc are also present throughout.
- *La Haine* contains humour to lighten the tone of the film. Compare the opening sequence with the second section of the film, (Chapter 2 'The guys from the projects' on the DVD, or 10.38 minutes in on the video). This sequence shows two of the main characters in a humorous light. Students could compare the documentary look and style of most of the film with the style used in the more humorous sequences.

In 1990, Paris experienced a series of riots in the suburbs, triggered in part by high unemployment among teenagers of North African descent. The protagonists of the film are of different racial backgrounds: Vinz is Jewish, Said, North African and Hubert, Afro-Caribbean, and the film charts their reaction to the death of a fourth friend, a North African, shot by police during a riot.

In this respect, the narrative structure (see p38) is the reverse of *Do the Right Thing*. While the latter builds up towards a climax of a riot scene, based on racial and social conflict, *La Haine* explores the during and after of a similar event, without using the narrative technique of suspense. What it does instead – and this is where we may arrive at a broad distinction between French cinema and Hollywood – is to offer an exploration of character, motivation, situation, rather than try to resolve a narrative.

What do students make of the ending? They may feel the ambiguity of the ending lacks the resolution of conventional Hollywood narratives. Also, what about the presumed death of one of the lead characters? Is this surprising and does it in any way alter their view of the film?

La Haine also enables students to consider the concept of *auteur* (see pXX). Kassovitz has made a film based on personal vision, rather than the need to entertain. In doing so, he has brought the reality of such events in Paris to a wider audience and highlighted some aspects of inner-city life that are of universal relevance. To what extent, however, can Kassovitz be considered an *auteur*, given his limited work as a director?

Students could also consider the distribution of foreign-language films. *La Haine* was a co-production with Canal+, a company that, together with Pathé, enables British audiences to see a variety of French productions. The film was distributed in the UK by Metro Tartan, one of several specialists in foreign-language and art-house productions.

● Approaching French cinema 2: *Beau travail*

Why study *Beau travail*?

- *Beau travail* is on the A2 Film Studies specification for FS5 – Studies in World cinema, as a close study film (from June 2004).
- The film could form the basis of a research topic for students wishing to focus on a female director and/or France as a national cinema.
- It could also be useful for exam specifications where Women and Film is a topic, eg OCR A2 Media Studies Unit 2734: Critical Research Study on the topic of Women and Film.

Courtesy of *bfi* Stills

Beau travail

Following a screening of *Beau travail*, it would be interesting to gauge the reaction of students as a starting point for considering the market for Claire Denis's films, beyond France. Students may be surprised to hear that all of Denis's feature films have achieved consistent distribution in Europe and the USA, including her most recent film, *Vendredi soir* (2002).

Guy Austin (1996) provides some historical and cultural links between the disparate factions in French cinema, which we can use in considering the films of Claire Denis, as a woman working in the French film industry.

- As with the rest of the world, the film industry in France is male-dominated at most levels, including directors, producers, technicians etc;
- Despite this, women have enjoyed a higher profile in French cinema than in any other national film industry;
- France can claim the first woman director, Alice Guy, who was working in the 1900s, as well as the first feminist filmmaker, Germaine Dulac, in the 1920s.
- One of the lesser-known directors of the French New Wave is Agnes Varda, who is still working today;
- French political filmmaking in the 1960s and 1970s reflected an interest in feminist issues. This so-called women's cinema became diluted in the 1980s with the work of more commercially successful directors, and a backlash against the idea that clearly disparate films should be categorised under one heading;
- Female directors have worked largely outside the mainstream – their films are generally not easy to place in terms of genre or other conventions. In the case of Claire Denis, narrative is conveyed through imagery, rather than sequential events;

● The work of female directors is not generally well known beyond their own country. A notable exception is *Trois hommes et un couffin* by Coline Serreau made in 1985, re-made by Hollywood in 1987 as *Three Men and a Baby* (Leonard Nimoy). When a foreign release is achieved, it tends to be through the art-house circuit.

Claire Denis

Despite being well regarded at film festivals throughout the world, Claire Denis's work is less well known in the UK. Her debut film, *Chocolat* (1988, France/West Germany/Cameroon), emerged from her experiences of childhood in post-colonial Africa. Denis was brought to Paris at the age of 14, returning to Senegal as an adult. This experience led her to consider herself as 'rootless', a theme she explores in her films.

Chocolat, directed and written by Denis, is one of several films made by women that explores the ex-colonial experience of women. Told in flashback by the narrator of the story, named France, it relates the story of her mother's infatuation with the family's black servant.

Denis continues the theme of France's colonial past and its legacy in *Beau Travail*. The main character, Galoup, played by Denis Lavant, describes himself as 'unfit for civilian life', having apparently known nothing but a tight-knit community of a former French colony on the northeast coast of Africa (since 1977, the Republic of Djibouti).

There are a number of elements that students could explore in relation to the film:

● *Beau travail* immerses the viewer in the world of the French Foreign Legion, as seen from the point of view of Galoup, who is devoted to his CO, Bruno Forestier (Michel Subor). Galoup thrives on routine and the restricted environment in which he serves, in contrast to the way he seems out of place when walking the streets of Marseilles. He maintains a constant military style in the way he dresses and behaves, and never seems to take time off.

● While Galoup is shown as isolated and detached, accepting that the military is his life and will follow the same pattern until the end, Denis depicts the soldiers who work under his command as a collective unit, working and socialising together in a spirit of co-dependency, with a sense that their future is open-ended.

● Galoup is in love with one of the African prostitutes (although there is no indication that she is interested in him, illustrated in the opening scene of the film).

● There is a strong homoerotic element running through the film. Denis arguably objectifies the male body; the soldiers become part of the *mise en scène*, blending with the landscape. Some of the most striking scenes in this beautiful film are during the training where Galoup choreographs a military exercise as if it were a ballet.

- The dialogue throughout is spare. Denis has expressed her opinion that there is too much explanatory dialogue in French cinema, so much in her film is conveyed visually and through character development. The film is beautiful to look at – a work of art – in its use of colour, pace and choice of location. It has the look of a tableau of images which piece together events, situations, some of narrative significance, others character revealing. In some ways the film makes more sense if it is thought of as a series of flashbacks from Galoup's memory.

Students may wish to investigate these themes further through textual analysis of *Beau travail* and to explore some of the representational issues emerging from the text. **Worksheet 16** contains suggestions on how to approach what may be viewed as a more challenging film.

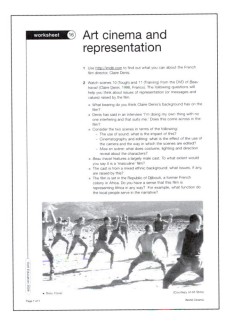

• Other issues to explore

- Claire Denis's background allows us to consider other representational issues in her films, particularly national identity. The settings of *Beau travail* and her earlier film, *Chocolat*, reflect a childhood spent in both Africa and France. Her films are marked by her strong nostalgia for the experience of living in Africa, combined with a sense of 'otherness', which set her and her family apart from the country they inhabited. The characters in both these films convey a sense of 'otherness', and we gain little insight into the African national perspective or any real sense of the environment that the characters occupy, which seems to provide no more than a suitable landscape to enhance the narrative and visual style of the films.

- Students may wish to consider Denis as a female film director, but arguably not a feminist one. Consider how *Beau travail* offers a different perspective on masculinity, picking up on ideas about how male and female audiences may be positioned to view these characters. Inevitably, Claire Denis is often asked about her experience as a French female film director and the extent to which her marginality is as a result of this.

No, I don't think I make the sort of films which have the characteristic traits of French cinema, which is to say a lot of dialogue and a very social focus. Some suggest my marginality has to do with the fact that my films have a lot of marginal characters in them. But I don't think so, I think it's more that I don't express myself like mainstream French directors. But being marginalized is a way of being slightly protected – I'm doing my own thing with no one interfering and that suits me. (Darke, 2000, p18)

● To what extent can Denis be considered an *auteur* (pp38–41). She works with a consistent team (co-screenwriter Jean-Pol Fargeau and Agnès Godard as cinematographer), which helps her to present a signature style with themes she has developed over time, largely emerging from personal experience.

● Comparisons can be made to the work of the British director Terence Davies, whose films *Distant Voices, Still Lives* (1988, UK) and *The Long Day Closes* (1992, UK) offer a selective piecing together of childhood memories through a series of tableau images. These serve to convey a sense of childhood, rather than an accurate, factual account of the childhood itself.

● See **Worksheets 17** and **18** for further activities on *Beau travail* and French film.

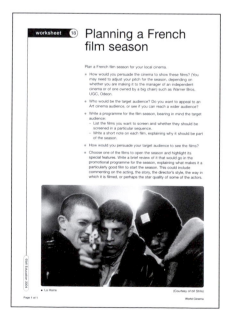

● Summary

French cinema can be considered:

- As a cinema with a consistent export history to the rest of the world;
- As a cinema undergoing transition, from the rural/historical phase of the 1980s to the social issues films of the 1990s.

Students could also consider:

- The release of films such as *La Haine* and the extent to which these are films emerging from a national cinema;
- Claire Denis as a case study of an *auteur* working within Art cinema, with its attendant restrictions and freedoms;
- A case study of a female but not overtly feminist director.

These issues can be adapted to study other well-established European cinemas.

Glossary

Alternative
In the context of World cinema, it is usually cited as the opposite of mainstream cinema, referring to films that offer an alternative use of film form or represent different ideological perspectives.

Art cinema
Typically applied to non-commercial, non-mainstream films, often from the European 'art-house' circuit; these may be challenging in subject matter or experimental in style, narrative form and genre. Distributors tend to target a niche audience who are interested in innovative and experimental approaches to filmmaking.

Audience
In Media Studies, the emphasis tends to be how an audience is targeted by media producers, or on reception theory, ie how an audience 'receives' a text (such as the effects on audiences of violent films). Film Studies tends to emphasise the individual experience of watching a film, spectatorship (see separate listing), as well as the site and condition of viewing (multiplex, art-house cinema etc).

Auteur
A director whose collective work features consistency of style, theme or approach, privileged over genre or narrative. The time and place in which the *auteur* is working is significant, often leading to subsequent reappraisal of her or his work. The concept of *auteur* has long been a subject for debate among film theorists as it tends to emphasise the director's input over that of other creative personnel. In World cinema, *auteur* theory tends to be more prevalent, then in relation to the genre-/industry-based films of Hollywood (although there are particular US filmmakers who are considered to be *auteurs*).

Avant-garde

Literally meaning 'front guard' and originally a military term; used to describe art forms (fine art, sculpture, literature, theatre, cinema etc) that are at the forefront of opposition to establishment forms. The history of international cinema has been characterised by various examples of avant-garde filmmaking (expressing a challenge to establishment cinema in terms of ideology and use of film form), often connected with art or political movements, such as Dadaism or feminism.

Binary opposition

Used to describe the use of polar opposites as a structuring device in art, literature and media, such as day/night, good/evil, male/female, black/white etc. Claude Lévi-Strauss originally used the idea in his work as an anthropologist and adopted by structural theorists.

Cinematic New Waves

Generally used to describe a group of films emerging at certain times out of specific cultural and historical contexts. Two of the most prominent of these are the French New Wave of Paris in the late1950s and the Hong Kong New Wave, at the time of Hong Kong's reunification with China. More recently, Mexican and Latin American New Wave cinemas have been identified.

Cultural imperialism

The domination by large US-based corporations of international markets, especially in the areas of food, fashion, music and popular entertainment, which often undermines the cultural status and economic viability of indigenous producers. This dominance is equated with more traditional kinds of imperialism or colonisation, whereby one country takes over another politically and militarily. In the case of cultural imperialism, dominance is achieved by economics and popular culture, often with the complicity of the indigenous audience. Also see Hegemony.

Discourse

Discourse is the expression of a point of view. The terms dominant, subordinate and radical can also be used to describe a discourse. When used in a cultural or ideological context, it frequently refers to the fact that the discourse in, for example, a film text, emanates from a dominant position or ideology, such as that of Hollywood and US culture. In World cinema, filmmakers from different countries may present a discourse from a subordinate or radical position, related to their particular culture or ideological perspective (eg a feminist or post-colonial discourse). Some of the more subtle aspects of this relate to the way power is used to control a discourse and to position an audience.

Distribution

The process by which films are rented from the production company to the exhibitor, including the circulation of film prints as well as the rights to sell the film on video/DVD, television etc.

Ethnocentrism

The use of one's own culture, or ethnicity, to judge another person's/country's. Frequently this term (and its variants, such as Eurocentrism) is used to discuss issues of ideology and is related to the concepts of cultural imperialism and representation, chiefly in respect of the (mis)apprehension that one's own culture is superior.

European cinema

A generalised term often used to classify cinema in opposition to 'Hollywood' in terms of audience, with films classified as being part of Art cinema (see separate listing). The category is problematic as it includes very diverse cinemas.

Exhibition

The process by which films are released according to a schedule and screened at cinemas.

Film grammar and style

The established conventions of the language of film (that are created by the constituents of moving images and sound) and the devices at its disposal, eg the meaning introduced the organising principles, or grammar, of genre and narrative. For example, genre conventions can only work (or be subverted) if the rules are correctly displayed and interpreted by film and spectator.

Globalisation

Marshal McLuhan's prediction in the 1960s of a 'global village' is taken for granted in the 21st century world of mass communication. The globalisation of culture refers to the omnipresence of recognised brands, and the globalisation of the media refers to the convergence of companies and their products. For example, international media ownership is chiefly concentrated in the hands of the 'Big Six': Viacom, Bertelsmann AG, Disney, News Corporation, Vivendi Universal and AOL-Time-Warner.

Hegemony

Derived from the work of Italian political thinker and Marxist Antonio Gramsci, hegemony refers to the power that a strong social group exerts to create a consensus which makes their status seem natural, common-sense and legitimate. It is often used to describe the powerful effect of Hollywood mainstream cinema, whose use of film form and ideology (ideas, values and beliefs) seems the only or best way to make films. This hegemony of Hollywood, it is argued, makes it difficult for audiences to enjoy and appreciate any other kinds of cinema, even indigenous films.

Heterogeneous/homogeneous

Two useful terms used to describe the representation of people, their culture and ideology. Heterogeneity, being the opposite of homogeneity, describes the differences in any given constituency, ie all women are not the same, all Americans are not the same, all people of colour are not the same. In ideological analyses of Hollywood films, it is often asserted that dominant cinema tends to reinforce homogeneity, whereas World cinema emphasises difference, contradiction and plurality.

Independent/'indie'

The term referred originally to film production companies that were independent of the Hollywood studio system. In contemporary Hollywood, however, very few filmmakers are completely independent from some aspect of the Hollywood production, distribution or exhibition process. So the term – especially the abbreviation 'indie' – is now frequently used to describe a style of film, typically aimed at either a young or art-house audience, perhaps with low production values or self-consciously formal techniques. The term is similarly applied to some genres of contemporary music, where true independence from major record labels is rare, but 'indie' describes a style of music appealing to a niche audience.

Indigenous

Belonging to the country of origin under discussion.

Mainstream

Usually referring to popular cinema.

Movement

A political or artistic phenomenon where several individuals unite to develop an idea, policy or art form at the same time, sometimes related to the avant-garde or underground. The history of film is punctuated with specific movements, such as Russian Formalism, Italian Neo-Realism, Surrealism, German Expressionism, film noir, French New Wave, British Free Cinema etc.

'Other'

This is a relativist concept, used to describe individuals or social groups who are the opposite of 'us'. It is often used in a binary opposition, according to the status of the person who is identifying the difference, so it is frequently used to express the difference between gender, race, nationality, colour etc. In an African film, a white, Western character would represent the 'other', for example.

Post-colonialism

Usually a critique of the colonial power implicit in many examples of World cinema, including Australian, New Zealand and African cinema, for example.

Realism

This complex term (with its origins, as social realism, in literature and fine art) is charged with a variety of aesthetic and political associations. It is the attempt, in a constructed text, to recreate a sense of reality and believability by the use of technical codes and relationships, values and beliefs. It is also a relative term, as we do not all share the same perception of reality, hence multiple and different realities may be represented. Realism is the dominant mode of representation in all categories and forms of media texts. In *La Haine*, for example, a 'documentary look' (achieved by hand-held camera, grainy film stock, natural or naturalistic lighting, and ambient sound) is used in a fictional film to create a heightened sense of immediacy and believability.

Representation (messages and values, ideology)

Closely related to realism, this term refers to the fact that, when shown in the media, all events, people, places are mediated by the media form and its producers – what we watch, read or listen to is not real, but something that stands for, or *re*-presents, that reality. How these representations are interpreted depends on the audience's, or spectator's, view of the world, which in turn is based on their personal ideas, values and beliefs (ideology). Any representation has the power to educate, inform or misinform. In World cinema, self-representation is a key issue: indigenous filmmakers are in the best position to represent their own culture and people most fairly and accurately. National cinemas thus have a crucial role to play in representing a nation and its experience back to its people.

Spectatorship

The consideration of how audiences are 'positioned' by the inner workings of the film text. This is of particular interest in World cinema, as the intended indigenous audience can take a very different spectator 'position' to an audience beyond the film's country of origin.

Stars

A signifying system which is open to interpretation across different cultures: a Hollywood star is 'reappraised' when appearing in a European film; similarly, British actors enjoy the 'status' of stars because of their profile in Hollywood films.

Third cinema

Coined in 1969 by two Argentinian filmmakers, Fernando Solanas and Octavio Getino. According to them Hollywood is first cinema, European *auteurs* and art cinema are second cinema. Third cinema consists of films from countries outside the two main dominant sources of international power. It advocates decolonisation of culture through a counter-cinema, ie one that subverts, or offers alternatives to, dominant cinema (Hollywood) in the use of film form and representation of ideological perspectives etc.

Third World cinema

This term originally derived from the categorisation of countries according to a world order of power and influence, so that the West was the First World, the East, the Second and the rest, the Third World. In the Cold War, the term was used to describe countries that were not directly aligned with either of the two superpowers, the USA and the former Soviet Union. However, it has also become synonymous with what we now call the countries of the developing world, principally those of the African continent; however, the term 'World cinema' is often used in preference to it.

World cinema

World cinema comprises the output of individual national cinemas and frequently is used to describe non-Hollywood films. Present in many national cinemas is the theme of post-colonialism, the revisiting and exploration of a nation's history, in particular its former relationships with a colonial country, such as Great Britain, France, Portugal etc.

Bibliography and filmography

References

G Austin (1996), *Contemporary French Cinema*, Manchester University Press

P Buddrus, 'Moodysson Follows up on Early Promise', at
www.screendaily.com

S Chau (2001), '*Crouching Tiger* makes history in Hong Kong', at
www.screendaily.com.

F Dannen and B Long (1997), *Hong Kong Babylon: An Insider's Guide to the
Hollywood of the East*, Faber and Faber

C Darke (2000), 'Desire Is Violence', *Sight and Sound,* July

R Dyer (1979), *Stars*, bfi Publishing

E Dyja (ed) (2001), *BFI Film and Television Handbook 2002*, bfi Publishing

J Forbes and S Street (2000), *European Cinema*, Palgrave

S Hayward (1997), *Key Concepts in Cinema Studies*, Routledge

J Hill and P Church Gibson (1998), *The Oxford Guide to Film Studies,* OUP

K Jackson (1998), *The Language of Cinema,* Carcanet

M Kermode (2001), 'Banned Back Stories: *The Idiots* Uncut', at
www.filmfour.com/banned

G Macnab (2001), 'House Rules', *Sight and Sound*, June

L Mulvey (1975), 'Visual Pleasure and Narrative Cinema', *Screen*, vol 16, no 3

G Nowell-Smith (ed) (1997), *The Oxford History of World Cinema,* OUP

L Odham Stokes and M Hoover (2001), *City on Fire*, Verso

J Pym (ed) (2003), *Time Out Film Guide,* Penguin

T Rayns (1995), 'Poet of Time', *Sight and Sound,* September

T Rayns (2000), 'Charisma Express', *Sight and Sound,* January

T Rayns (2000), 'In the Mood for Edinburgh', *Sight and Sound,* August

K Reader (1995), 'After the Riot', *Sight and Sound*, November

G Roberts and H Wallis (2001), *Introducing Film*, Arnold

L Shackleton (2002), 'Warner Bros. Makes First Foray into Chinese-Language Film Production' at www.screendaily.com

L Shackleton (2003), 'China to Lift Quota Restrictions for Hong Kong Films' at www.screendaily.com

S Teo (2001), *Hong Kong Cinema, bfi*

Recommended further reading and viewing

It would be impossible to provide a comprehensive list of all that World cinema has to offer. Instead, I have restricted suggestions to mainly contemporary films, using the subjects featured in this resource as a frame of reference. Recommended reading includes the publications and websites listed in the Bibliography.

● Hong Kong cinema

Films

- Other films to help consider Wong Kar-Wai as an *auteur* in addition to *Chungking Express* and *In the Mood for Love* (the DVD extras for this film are particularly good) as well as providing examples of Art cinema:
  - *As Tears Go by* (1988, Hong Kong)
  - *Days of Being Wild* (1991, Hong Kong)
  - *Ashes of Time* (1994, Hong Kong/China/Taiwan)
  - *Fallen Angels* (1995, Hong Kong)
  - *Happy Together* (1997, Hong Kong)
- Hong Kong action films directed by John Woo, also considered to be an *auteur*, which have enjoyed mainstream success:
  - *A Better Tomorrow* (1986, Hong Kong)
  - *The Killer* (1989, Hong Kong)
  - *Bullet in the Head* (1990, Hong Kong)
  - *Hard-Boiled* (1992, Hong Kong)

Books

F Dannen and B Long (1997), *Hong Kong Babylon: An Insider's Guide to the Hollywood of the East*, Faber and Faber

J Hill and P Church Gibson (1998), *The Oxford Guide to Film Studies,* OUP

L Odham Stokes and M Hoover (2001), *City on Fire*, Verso

S Teo (2001), *Hong Kong Cinema*, bfi

● Swedish and Danish cinema

Films

● Other films by Lars von Trier in addition to *The Idiots*:
  – *Europa* (1991, Denmark/Sweden/France/Germany/Switzerland)
  – *Breaking the Waves* (1996, Denmark/Sweden/France/Netherlands/ Norway)
  – *Dogville* (2003, Denmark/Sweden/France/Norway/Netherlands/Finland/ Germany/Italy/Japan/USA/UK)

● Other films by Lukas Moodysson in addition to *Show Me Love*:
  – *Together* (2000, Sweden/Denmark/Italy)
  – *Lilya 4-Ever* (2002, Sweden/Denmark)

● Films by Thomas Vinterberg:
  – *Festen* (1998, Denmark/Sweden)
  – *It's All about Love* (2003, USA/Japan/Sweden/UK/Denmark/Germany/ Netherlands)

Books

J Hill and P Church Gibson (1998), *The Oxford Guide to Film Studies*, OUP

M Hjort and S. MacKenzie (eds), *Purity and Provocation: Dogma 95*, *bfi* Publishing

G Nowell-Smith (ed) (1997), *The Oxford History of World Cinema*, OUP

J Rockwell (2003), *The Idiots*, *bfi* Modern Classics*, bfi* Publishing

J Stevenson (2002), *Lars von Trier*, *bfi* World Directors, *bfi* Publishing

● French Cinema

Films

● Films which offer a comparison with *La Haine*, as suggested under the section on French cinema:
  – *Do the Right Thing* (Spike Lee, 1989, USA)

- *Les Nuits fauves* (Cyril Collard, 1992, France/Italy)
- Other films by Claire Denis in addition to *Beau Travail*:
  - *Chocolat* (1998, France/West Germany/Cameroon)
  - *Vendredi soir* (2002, France) as an example of 'European cinema' as 'Art cinema'

- Films by directors of the French New Wave, including:
  - *À Bout de souffle* (Jean-Luc Godard, 1960, France)
  - *Les Quatre cents coups* (François Truffaut, 1959, France)

Books

G Austin (1996), *Contemporary French Cinema*, Manchester University Press

J Forbes and S Street (2000), *European Cinema*, Palgrave

J Hill and P Church Gibson (1998), *The Oxford Guide to Film Studies,* OUP

G Nowell-Smith (ed) (1997), *The Oxford History of World Cinema,* OUP

R Stafford (2000), *York Film Notes on* La Haine, Longman

M Temple and M Witt (eds) (2003), *French Cinema Book*, *bfi* Publishing

G Vincendeau (2003), *Jean-Pierre Melville: An American in Paris*, *bfi* Publishing

● General reading

Magazines/journals

Screen – specialist cinéaste/academic journal –
http://www3.oup.co.uk/screen

Sight and Sound monthly magazine (*bfi* Publishing) – essential reading for up-to-date coverage of World cinema, with a discounted subscription for students – **www.bfi.org.uk/sightandsound**

Kamera – published five times per year, available by subscription and in specialist bookshops – **www.kamera.co.uk**, with a special emphasis on World cinema and cult films/directors

bfi Education *Media Briefing: The Global Picture* –
www.bfi.org.uk/mediabriefing

Teaching guides

R Ashbury, W Helsby and M O'Brien (1999), *Teaching African Cinema*, *bfi* Teaching Guide – book
W Hewing (2003), *British Cinema in the 1960s*, *bfi* Teaching Guide – CD-Rom
M O'Brien and K Withall (2002), *Bollywood and Beyond*, *bfi* Teaching Guide – CD-Rom and VHS tape

Books

The general film studies titles above and below contain useful bibliographies for further research. The books on specific national cinemas below are only a selection, and your attention is drawn to the BFI online research resources for access to a more comprehensive collection.

bfi Library resources

The *bfi* Library has several online bibliographies (free to download) which would be essential in the preparation for teaching any aspect of World cinema or to support students' independent research:

16+ guides

www.bfi.org.uk/nationallibrary/collections/16+
These include resources on:

- *Auteur* theory/*Auteurs*
- Contemporary British cinema
- Iranian cinema
- South Asian film/TV
- Contemporary European cinema

Annotated bibliographies

www.bfi.org.uk/nationallibrary/collections/bibliographies/index.html
These include resources on:

- African films/TV
- Mexican and Chicano cinema

bfi National Library – search facility for films, books, journals, stills etc – an essential academic resource: **http://lib.bfi.org.uk/cgi-bin/w207.sh**

- *General Film Studies books*

N Abrahams, I Bell and J Udris (2001), *Studying Film*, Arnold – includes a chapter on national cinemas and film movements

G Andrew (ed) (2001), *Film: The Critic's Choice*, Aurum Press

P Cook and M Biernink (eds) (1999), *The Cinema Book*, *bfi* Publishing

M Hjort and S MacKenzie (2000), *Cinema and Nation*, Routledge

A Kuhn and S Radstone (eds) (1990), *The Women's Companion to International Film*, Virago

J Nelmes (ed) (2003), *An Introduction to Film Studies*, 3rd edn, Routledge – contains a large section on national cinemas

J Pym (ed) (2002) *Time Out Film Guide* (published annually), Penguin. Probably one of the best film reference guides in terms of coverage of World cinema. The appendices provide comprehensive listings by country, director, actor and general subject headings. This would be useful for some of the activities suggested in this resource

G Turner (2000), *Film as Social Practice*, Routledge – has a chapter on national film, ideology and culture

The *bfi* publishes a series, World Directors, which includes titles on Jane Campion, Lars von Trier, Youssef Chahine, Yash Chopra, Emir Kusturica and Terrence Malick

● *Australia and New Zealand*

T O'Reagan (2001), *Australian National Cinema*, Routledge

J Rayner (2000), *Contemporary Australian Cinema: An Introduction*, MUP

J Robson and B Zalcock (1997), *Girls' Own Stories: Australian and New Zealand Women's Films*, Scarlett Press

● *British and Irish cinema*

Y Allon, D Cullen and H Patterson (eds) (2001), *Contemporary British and Irish Directors*, Wallflower Press

J Caughie and K Rockett (1996), *The Companion to British and Irish Cinema*, Cassell/*bfi*

E Dyja (2003), *The BFI Film and Television Handbook*, *bfi* Publishing

M McLoone (2001), *Irish Film: The Emergence of a Contemporary Cinema*, *bfi* Publishing

D Petrie (2000), *Screening Scotland*, *bfi* Publishing

P Wickham (2003), *Producing the Goods?: British Film Production since 1990* – a *bfi* Information Briefing, *bfi* Publishing

● *Eastern Europe*

M Haltof (2002), *Polish National Cinema*, Berghahn Books

R Taylor, N Wood, J Graffy and D Iordanova (2003), *The BFI Companion to Eastern European and Russian Cinema, bfi* Publishing

● *Europe*

A Jäckel (2003), *European Film Industries*, *bfi* Publishing

- *Germany*

T Bergfelder, E Carter and D Gokturk (2003), *The German Cinema Book, bfi* Publishing

T Elsaesser and M Wedel (2003), *The BFI Companion to German Cinema, bfi* Publishing

- *Spain*

B Jordan and R Morgan-Tamosunas (1998), *Contemporary Spanish Cinema*, MUP

N Triana-Toribio (2003), *Spanish National Cinema*, Routledge

- *Japan*

D Richie (2001), *100 Years of Japanese Film*, Kodansha International

M Schilling (1999), *Contemporary Japanese Film*, Weatherhill

● Useful websites

www.bbfc.co.uk – the British Board of Film Classification website. Includes search facility for the classification of foreign language films prior to release in the UK

www.bfi.org.uk – the British Film Institute website. Also contains listings for the National Film Theatre in London and is an invaluable resource for World cinema films

www.bfi.org.uk/sightandsound – a searchable database of all published reviews, synopses, credits and features published in *Sight and Sound* magazine

www.dfi.dk – website for the Danish Film Institute. Contains search facility for Danish production companies and forthcoming releases, as well as archive material

www.filmunlimited.org.uk – excellent film website for *The Guardian*

www.kamera.co.uk – an excellent film site, a companion to the magazine *Kamera*, with features, reviews and interviews on World cinema and cult films/directors

www.kinoeye.org.uk – includes e-mail list offering news from film festivals, as well as perspectives on less well known aspects of European film. Subjects include the films of the former Yugoslav republics

www.mediasalles.it – an industry website originating in Italy which aims to increase awareness of Europe's cinema cultures, as well as providing statistical data on the European film industry

www.moviem.co.uk – a website that specialises in selling World cinema DVD/VHS titles, including the *bfi*'s Connoisseur label, which is a major label for World cinema titles

www.screendaily.com – website for *Screen International* magazine with a facility to receive daily e-mails with news stories about future productions, box-office performance etc – subscription only

www.screenonline.org.uk – an unprecedented website resource from the *bfi* which includes a video and sound archive (free to institutional organisations), with tours/commentaries, on British cinema from 1890 to the present day

www.sensesofcinema.com – an excellent Australian film site, with reviews, features and interviews, which has profiles on many World cinema *auteurs*, including Lars von Trier and Wong Kar-Wai

www.sfi.se – Swedish Film Institute website. Provides up-to-date information on the Swedish film industry, with an emphasis on production and box-office data

www.unifrance.org – has the aim of promoting French cinema worldwide. Of particular interest are the sections 'Careers of French Films Abroad' and 'Careers of French Films in France' which provide information on festivals, films in pre-production, forthcoming releases, box-office performance

Acknowledgments

I would like to thank my students and colleagues at East Surrey College (Redhill in Surrey, UK) for being the inspiration behind the writing of this guide.

Thanks also to Vivienne Clark for her support and encouragement throughout and to Wendy Earle at the *bfi*.

I would like to dedicate this book to Kevin Gamm.